LAYING UP YOUR BOAT

Other titles in the *Sailmate* series

The *Sailmate* series provides practical information on specific topics at an affordable price.

How to Trim Sails
Peter Schweer
ISBN 0 7136 3323 9
A practical guide to getting the optimum from your sails. It covers the equipment necessary for sail trimming, as well as tuning the rig for varying conditions. Masthead, swept-spreader, fractional, fractional with running backstays and dinghy rigs are all covered in this handy pocket guide. Easy reference trimming tables are also included.

How to Use Radar
H. G. Strepp
ISBN 0 7136 3324 7
This book explains all the latest in radar technology, including how different types of sets work, how they should be operated and the use of radar for both navigation and collision avoidance. Examples are all based on the most up-to-date equipment.

Other *Sailmate* titles in preparation:

Heating and Cooling Systems
E. Lamprecht
ISBN 0 7136 3528 2

How to Design a Boat
John Teale
ISBN 0 7136 3529 0

LAYING UP YOUR BOAT

———— H. Janssen ————

ADLARD COLES NAUTICAL
LONDON

Published by Adlard Coles Nautical
an imprint of A & C Black (Publishers) Ltd
35 Bedford Row, London WC1R 4JH

ISBN 0-7136-3456-1

A CIP catalogue record for this book is available
from the British Library.

Translated from the German edition by
Robin Inches, MITI.

Photographs: Hans-Günter Kiesel (2),
Helge Janssen (30).
Drawings: Helge Janssen.

Printed and bound in Great Britain by
J. W. Arrowsmith Ltd., Bristol BS3 2NT

Contents

Contents

Contents

About this book

When winter arrives in the north, our boats and yachts disappear into boatsheds, under tarpaulins or tube and canvas structures. A proud yacht in laid-up condition – wrapped and firmly tied like a mummy, emptied of gear, cold and dank – is not only a depressing sight but is also extremely uncomfortable; many owners just forget all about their beloved floating 'home from home' until next spring approaches.

And why not? After all, the craft is resting safely in its storage cradle. If the worst should happen – such as damage from storm, fire or even theft – the insurance will take care of it. What little maintenance work is needed, such as repainting the hull and revarnishing the cockpit gratings, can surely be done a few days before recommissioning. And anyway, what can go wrong with a modern plastic hull yacht with galvanised or stainless steel rigging, stainless steel fittings, Dacron sails and a diesel engine?

However, many a boatowner who divides the year into two halves in this way (and even believes that the boat is being preserved since it is ageing at only half the rate of, say, a car that is in use all year) has failed to take account of 'the sharp tooth of time' that gnaws away at the boat.

In this respect, boatowners in warmer climates are substantially better off in a number of ways. Firstly, for them a long active season is followed by only a short laying-up period, which isn't even a true one: along the Med, in Florida, the Caribbean and the South Seas a large majority of yachts remain in the water fully rigged all year round, merely being slipped briefly once or twice to repaint the underwater hull.

So a yacht in the south 'notices' that it is laid up only by the fact that its owner doesn't show up on board during the cooler months; at best a paid watchman occasionally does the rounds to check the hatches and pump out the bilges. But even here time is gnawing away – both at the boat and at the bank balance. In fact, it is probably gnawing even more keenly than where winter weather forces owners to take an intensive interest in their boats at least twice a year.

Doubtless you see your yacht or motorboat as an investment, one that cost a lot of money to buy and should last you for as long as possible and still hold its value. If so, you will surely wish to keep this investment well maintained and in the best operating condition for the maximum possible length of time, to obtain many years of pleasure from it.

That's where this book will help, because it provides you with valuable advice and suggestions. It will not only tell you how to bring your boat ashore safely, prop it up and cover it effectively, but you will also find out how to prepare the boat, its technical equipment and all its accessories for winter so as to minimize the damage from condensation and damp, rust and rot, corrosion, wind, ice and snow.

Because this book lists everything that owners can do to help their boats come safely through the winter, it may be that your conscience will prick you when you read it because up till now you haven't been putting in even half the effort described here. I have allowed for that and anticipated it; I've even intended you to react this way. But I am also aware that for reasons of time, money or whatever, you will ignore certain tasks and apply priorities when it comes to working on your boat during the winter. So I suggest that you just select from this book whatever you reckon you have to do to be satisfied every spring that you have a well-tended, sound, seaworthy and safe craft.

I wish you great success and I wish your boat the proper tending it deserves in its winter quarters.

Helge Janssen

Laying up for the winter

Laying up in a warm climate

In the sunny climates, where even during the winter months it neither freezes nor snows, everything is different. During the cool seasons of the year the harbours and marinas along the Mediterranean coast, in the Caribbean, the Pacific, South Africa or Australian waters, often differ very little in appearance from the summer months because most boats remain in the water the whole year round. Only a few owners bring their craft ashore to protect them for at least a few months from damage from swell that might affect the harbour during storms. Even then, masts and rigging are left standing; very often, just the sails are removed and the engines protected against corrosion.

For those boats that remain in the water, generally no more is done than during the active season: inspection and maintenance are carried out fairly regularly, involving running the engine occasionally, recharging the batteries on board, pumping out the bilges, airing the below-deck compartments, and checking the mooring arrangements. Since boats – whether ashore (the few) or afloat (the many) – during this time of idleness continue to be exposed to the weather – and, above all, to the sun – they suffer substantially from the effects of atmospheric exposure. You could even say that craft in warm climates age a great deal faster than those in the chilly north because they are constantly exposed to the elements.

Routine maintenance for Med yachts mostly concerns only the underwater hull, which once or twice a year has to have the growth removed and a fresh coat of antifouling applied. The opportunity is often taken at this point to renew the prop shaft stern gland seal, repair rudder and hull penetration fittings if necessary, and give the outer surface of the hull a fresh protective coat of wax. Time on the slip is expensive, so more comprehensive tasks, like removing the old coats of antifouling, filling and sanding work, dealing with osmosis and repairing keel damage after grounding, are often neglected until the extent of the damage necessitates a proper (and thus even more expensive) spell in a yard.

Owners have even less chance of attending to the rigging and other technical equipment on board. The most that can be done with standing rigging is to carry out superficial checks where at best visible broken wires, rubbed places, worn halyard blocks and damaged running rigging will be discovered. The condition of bottlescrews or terminals on shrouds and stays can only be established by dismantling them; the condition of through-mast bolts, for example in the spreader and masthead areas, will only be discovered by complete de-rigging.

What applies to the boat and its rigging applies even more strongly to the on-board technical equipment. Maintenance and servicing for auxiliary engines means an engine-oil change and renewal of engine oil, fuel and, if applicable, coolant filters; other tasks, such as cleaning/descaling the cooling circuit, checking the diesel engine injectors by removing and pressure testing them, are often omitted until a defect arises.

It's much the same with electrics and electronics; the equipment is scarcely ever removed for lengthy periods of disuse, thus it remains exposed the whole year round to the aggressive humidity of salt water.

Yachts in the Med, many of whose owners live hundreds of miles away and are unable to do much to care for and maintain their craft, have a comparatively short life expectancy unless they are looked after carefully by reliable experts on the spot.

Not only does that cost a lot of money, but in many places such care is simply not given because of a lack of experts, efficient boatyards or even interest. Our just demands of thoroughness from foreign mechanics, fitters, electricians, painters, riggers, sailmakers, boat builders and harbourmasters are often beyond their experience and ability. This is why many boats in southern harbours resemble sorry hulks after only five years: neglected, worn out, and no longer seaworthy.

Owners of large vessels tend to employ a boatkeeper for good reason. Owners who can't afford that luxury, and furthermore believe they can save themselves the expense of laying up, pay heavily for this – especially when selling their boats. These boats are offered in the yachting magazine advertisements often at lower prices than boats from northern waters. The laying-up situation is not quite so critical for charter yachts in southern waters available from the really good and efficient charterers. Many not only have their own bases with expert staff; but they are also compelled to meet the exacting standards of their customers by supplying high-quality boats if they wish to remain successful in the charter business. For that reason, charter yachts are often cared for and maintained much better than private boats, including during the 'winter' when for three or four months there are no customers and the boats are thoroughly overhauled in preparation for the coming season.

Laying up in warm regions, as we have seen, often does not occur. However, the advantages of cost savings and all the year round availability are often cancelled out by the massive disadvantages of high stress and rapid ageing of boats due to weathering, inadequate maintenance as a result of lack of time, and thus early loss of resale value. On balance, northern boats are better off – provided they receive expert laying-up treatment.

Laying up in a cold climate

When considering laying up in all its aspects we should include among the 'cold' regions not only those where snow and ice are the rule during the winter months. Thus this category includes all the countries around the English Channel, the North Sea and Baltic, as well as countries with milder climates around the Atlantic which, by virtue of the Gulf Stream, are generally subject to windy, raw weather with only occasional frosty spells: France, the Benelux countries and the United Kingdom.

In all these countries it is customary to lay up boats; indeed, this is considered a necessity. However, what it means in practice differs considerably from country to country. The reason for this is not only that the winter weather varies but also there are differences in personal attitudes towards the vessel.

Let's start with the Scandinavians. Anyone who has been sailing there in summer and has seen the enormous open spaces and 'boat parks' on the shoreside of yacht harbours will have no difficulty in imagining what things look like there in winter: indeed, almost all Scandinavian yachts are stored on hards immediately adjoining the harbour; permanent sheds for laying up are almost unknown. And many Nordic yacht owners don't even consider it necessary to cover their boat with tarpaulin to protect it from ice and snow – you see many boats with only the cockpit region covered and quite a few that are expected to withstand the blizzards without any protection at all. Scandinavian sailors simply have a different attitude; for them much more than for us the boat is just an item of sports equipment: an utensil in which you invest as little emotional involvement and money as possible.

Naturally, even boats constructed in modern synthetic materials suffer considerably from having their decks covered in ice and snow unless a protective coating of wax or synthetic resin has been applied carefully to seal them. But even that doesn't usually happen. In this way, the Scandinavians certainly save a lot of money on a roof structure or a weatherproof tarpaulin. And, on the face of it, they also save themselves time and worry because there is no need for frequent checks on the covering after winter gales.

The 'temperate' English, Scots, Irish, Dutch, Belgians and French are prepared to allow a bit more expense for laying up.

However, not all craft are lifted out of the water in these countries because the rise and fall of the tide and the Gulf Stream reduce the risk of berths freezing over. But whether afloat or in the open ashore, the boats are usually elaborately covered. The variations that arise here in terms of time and effort applied again depend on the relationship between owner and boat, and boatowners' attitudes. Whereas the 'laid-back' Latins are inclined to put up with a scratch or two on their boat, conservative Anglo-Saxons will invest more money and time in safely bringing their craft through the winter. Nevertheless, special laying-up sheds are rare, and British boatowners tend to lay up under tarpaulins.

In terms of laying up, we can learn a great deal from German procedures. No other country builds as many cantilevered sheds with composition or tarmac flooring; during the summer, these sheds are used for car parking or tennis, but in the winter they accommodate boats. Germany has excellent transport systems with travelhoists, hydraulic elevating trolleys and movable storage cradles to allow even large craft to be brought ashore rapidly – and with centimetre accuracy. There is rarely a boatowner anywhere else in the world who is as particular in his construction of a canvas roof, a tarpaulin housing or even a shed for his boat as a German sailing enthusiast.

To summarize: the obligation to lay up our boats in the north for four to six months, apart from a lot of drawbacks (short active season, additional cost and effort for laying up, non-utilized berthing facilities), brings with it many advantages for the vessel.

For example, the work of 'decommissioning', if carried out by owner and crew, provides a good opportunity for a precise assessment of the condition of a boat. That applies not only to the hull, but also to the rigging, the engine, and the remainder of the technical equipment on board.

Furthermore, the long period when the boat is laid up makes it possible to carry out at one's leisure thorough overhauls, conversion and installation work, and repairs and improvements. It is with regard to these questions and problems that this book is intended to help. For that reason, from here on we will quite specifically be dealing with laying up in the north. (This does not, however, mean that the owner of a boat in the Med cannot also pick up a tip or two.)

Laying up afloat

Laying up in this way does not really amount to true laying up, but is merely bringing a boat through the cold season (with a lot of savings by way of expense and effort, but also involving

One type of laying-up arrangement. A tarpaulin over the top and no need to worry further. Without doubt this is the worst solution to the problem, with damage to hull, rigging and radar guaranteed.

a lot of risks). The risks are obvious. The greatest hazard is the craft becoming frozen in the iced-up harbour if the winter is a harsh one. In the worst cases (when the hull sides are near to vertical in the waterline region), the ice around the vessel has to be removed at regular intervals to prevent ice pressure permanently damaging the hull. As is well known, water is at its maximum density at 4° Celsius; it expands again as its temperature drops further. The resulting ice not only bursts glass bottles, but can also crush even large ships – as we know from the early Arctic expeditions. The repeated (in severe frost perhaps even daily) freeing of the boat from the ice has to be effected by hacking away from on deck or with the aid of a technically elaborate automatic de-icing installation often used in Northern Europe but rarely needed in the UK. A perforated hose surrounding the hull, floating on the water and connected to a compressor, blows out air on demand (thermal- or time-switch) to inhibit freezing.

Owners of boats with the hull strongly curved at waterline level, or hard-chine with the chine above the waterline, don't need to worry as much about ice. The expansion of the ice will merely lift the hull somewhat and force it up out of the water. At the very least, that means damage to the underwater paint, and perhaps – in the case of GRP boats – to the gel coat which is the thin outer surface coating of the hull. However, should the ice (due to extreme cold) become thick enough to extend down to the steering gear (skeg, rudder blade), you will have to be prepared for serious damage.

Thus anyone determined to winter a craft at its berth – whether in order to sail at New Year, to save money on the crane, or because of a dislike of fixed dates for slipping – should be absolutely clear in their mind that a boat hull must not be allowed to set in ice. Hack it away laboriously or bubble it away expensively – but it must be removed!

Once that problem has been solved, owners have to give thought to the protection of their boat against ice and snow, gales and swell. Since the rigging of a yacht laid up afloat is usually left standing, it has to be the first part to receive attention: effective protection of a mast with its standing rigging is not possible unless mast, masthead with electronics, fittings and lights can be wrapped in something that can be relied on to keep out water. Water that freezes in the mast track, in sheave boxes, on the wind gauge, or in plug-in connectors of the mast electrics, always destroys component parts. And when it thaws, the lumps of ice that formed when the rain froze will drop off, making nasty holes in the deck and superstructure. So it can be seen that mast and rigging should be taken down and stored ashore.

The hull itself (after most things that are movable, including books, charts, seat cushions, navigational and technical equipment, have been removed and stored in a dry place) must be protected against ice and snow by a well-secured tarpaulin. This is because freezing water (boat enemy No 1 in winter) can do a lot of damage here also: everywhere there are openings, splits and joints, such as seams and minute tears in laid teak decking, bearings of the tiller or wheel steering gear, fittings, engine control levers, drainpipes from decks and cockpit (the latter with sea cocks); all of these are susceptible to the destructive force of ice. Even the best gel coat layer available is not complete protection against the moisture that enters the capillaries and penetrates down to the glass-mat reinforcement of the hull material. The tarpaulin should therefore cover the whole of the boat including the pulpit and pushpit and, if possible, also protect the hull sides by means of an appropriate overhang.

Finally, there is the question of how to protect one's boat in its winter berth against the danger arising from swell; this could batter the boat against quays or jetties. Here you must take into account the fact that synthetic-fibre rope and rubber fenders at low temperatures lose their elasticity and thus their effectiveness, and that pneumatic fenders, blown up hard in summer, become too flabby and thin to absorb shocks in winter. There is nothing for it but to use metal shock absorbers with (galvanized) coil springs, frequently pumped-up pneumatic fenders, and to make frequent personal checks.

Concerning break-ins, burglary, or even theft of the whole craft from its winter berth, you had better talk (beforehand) to your insurers. If they're prepared to insure you, and you're prepared to accept all the other disadvantages of the craft being laid up afloat, all well and good. One thing is clear though: the boat certainly won't look any better by the spring. It will in any case have to be brought ashore for a fresh coat of underwater paint and for some checks around the submerged part of the hull (prop, rudder, openings through the hull). So your only gain is that you save the cost of the winter berth ashore (and instead have to pay for one afloat?), don't need a storage cradle, and are totally free from any crane, shed or transport related problems such as fixed dates. But what price do you pay for this option?

Laying up ashore in the open

The most usual way of laying up craft from a certain size upwards is still to unrig the vessels in the autumn, get them out of the water, and transport them to open-air storage where, safely parked and covered over, they spend the winter. This form of storage, as a solution that lies between the extremes of laying up afloat and winter storage in a boatyard shed, offers many advantages. The cost is usually reasonable, provided the boat can remain in the immediate vicinity of the harbour, where transport costs for special vehicles, cranes, etc do not arise. Furthermore, work on the craft can be carried out at any time (and earlier too in mild winter or spring weather), since neither the sweating of the hulls usual in boatsheds, nor the neighbour next-but-one doing varnishing, nor the yard being closed at night hinder one. Many owners prefer their boats to lie outdoors because it's cheaper and it gives them more independence.

However, there are also some significant disadvantages. Because of the danger of rotting as a result of high humidity and the risk of theft, owners need to strip the boat of almost everything that's movable – thus resulting in storage problems at home.

Furthermore, to protect the boat against the ravages of the weather, a stout tarpaulin will be needed. Depending on finances, the solutions adopted range from mere 'wrapping up' of the yacht to the building of a comfortable mini-shed with a steel-tubing frame, sturdy enough to permit living on board. And finally, laying up in the open also gives rise to many a sleepless night in January storms: are the tarpaulin lashings holding, is there something that could chafe the hull skin, could the gale actually blow the boat over?

However, owners who 'take their boats home with them' – either on a specially licensed trailer towed behind a powerful car to their own piece of land, or by carrier to an open-air parking place near where they live – are, of course, better off. If you can see your boat by looking out of the window, or just nip over to it, you are to be envied.

A common sight: a badly secured tarpaulin cover blown off by the first storm.

But, the most important advantage of laying up ashore has still to be mentioned: it is the decommissioning, and the thorough checking linked to this, of all important parts of the craft and its equipment – the rigging, the engine and the various pieces of technology. This method also means that, in theory, one has a lot of time each year to repair or replace all the things that are worn out, broken or have been lost. This applies as much in the open as in the laying up shed, though of course in the latter everything is easier, more comfortable and safer.

Laying up ashore – in a club shed, the marina, or privately

Not all owners have the good fortune (and the means) to know that while a blizzard is howling outside, their boat is safe and sound in a sturdy and dry storage shed. In this respect, the most fortunate are those owners who belong to a (rare) club that has its own shed, and in which their vessels can pass the winter cheaply and in ideal conditions. Substantially more expensive, however, is laying up in a professionally run marina whose owner makes a living from servicing vessels.

Fitted in between these two options – both on a price and a quality basis – there are the private storage facilities for boats. Along many coasts and in harbours, farmers are offering their barns; construction firms hire out their storage sheds, and defunct factories let their workshops as laying-up facilities for boats. Such premises are not always completely rainproof and some have a sand floor; occasionally, they have neither power nor water. On the other hand, they tend to be fairly inexpensive and, as a rule, any work on the craft by oneself or by experts can be carried out at any time. And some of the private storers, recognizing a brand-new market, have acquired the know-how (and the technique) to supply transport both ways, setting up by experts, and to offer simple maintenance and overhaul services to the owners: tractors towing converted lorry chassis and

mast-carrying trailers made from steel tube welded together
are becoming a more common sight around yacht harbours in
the UK.

In this way, an estimated 10 to 15 per cent of all northern
boatowners enjoy the benefits of laying up under cover, which
we have already listed. Often it is possible to leave seat cushions,
books, charts, tools, lamps, sailbags, cordage and much more on
board, since the humidity in the shed is less than that outside.
Theft is less likely, as thieves would first need to break into the
shed. There is no need for an expensive tarpaulin and a structure
of appropriate strength to support it; a light plastic sheet laid
loosely over the boat is enough to protect it from the dust
resulting from neighbours' sanding. The winter's gales can
rattle the shed as much as they like; as long as it remains

This is one way of getting a lot of masts into winter quarters.
However, the masts have to have been de-rigged carefully, with
shrouds and stays securely lashed to them, to avoid chaos and
damage in the spring when the time comes to ship them out
again.

standing the vessel will come to no harm. Much of the work on board can be carried out at any time, regardless of rain, wind or snow. Usually, power and water are available. There is no need for the laborious clearing away of scaffolding, ladders, appliances and tools, and carefully re-securing the tarpaulin at the end of each day's work. However, set against these many advantages of laying up in an enclosed shed, there are also a few disadvantages to be aware of:

Fixed dates/times To maximize the use of space in a shed, it is usually necessary to set up the boats in a certain order. This means working to quite specific dates and times – often just twice yearly. By these dates/times, a boat must be de-rigged and prepared in the autumn; painting and repairing must be finished in the spring. Laying up in a club usually also means two days 'on duty' for all owners to cover arrival and departure.

Fire risk Should a laid-up boat catch fire, this rarely involves any risk other than for the immediate neighbours if it is kept in the open. In a shed, however, a burning vessel may cause a serious blaze which may – as has often been the case – destroy most or even all of the boats there. Incandescent material and poisonous fumes from GRP yachts, narrow spaces between the boats, exploding solvent and paint containers, full or (even worse!) nearly empty fuel tanks often mean failure in extinguishing a blaze in a laying-up shed. To reduce that risk, three things can be done (and are now often *required* by quite a few shed operators).

First, because lightweight dustsheets of wafer-thin PVC fly up from burning boats, waft across the shed and set fire to other vessels, low-flammability reinforced tarpaulins, obtainable from builders' merchants, should be used. Secondly, the fire can be tackled faster if every owner hangs a fire extinguisher over the side of his vessel: there should be one from every boat, chest-high. Thirdly, solvents and paints must be stored outside the shed, and soaked cleaning rags, paint brushes and open paint pots should not be permitted to be left around. Your only other aid – at least, in coping with the material loss – is a sound all-risks insurance (with a fixed rate).

Moisture from sweating This is quite a problem in laying-up sheds. If an icy-cold boat hull starts sweating when sun on the shed roof warms the air, you can't do any painting. This is most likely in the spring, a few days before your boat will be moved out, and you may wish to do last-minute maintenance. Condensation also forms in the compartments below deck. Obviously, there is no natural drying of the boats by the wind, so this has to be combated by means of dehumidifiers – containers with a special salt, obtainable from builders' merchants.

In spite of these disadvantages, laying up in a shed is a good idea. Preferably, of course, in your own club – since it is usually cheap and you are not dependent on the shed owner. If that is not possible, what about the option of taking your boat to a boatyard for laying up?

Laying up ashore – in an enclosed shed in a boatyard

This course of action is generally adopted by three categories of owners: those owning one or more boats for professional purposes (eg charterers and dealers); those unable to look after their vessel during the winter owing to lack of time or because they live a long way from the coast; and lastly, those sufficiently well off to do only the sailing but leave the problems of laying up and any necessary boat maintenance to the specialist staff of a boatyard.

In contrast to the clubs, marinas and private berths, the boatyard laying up sheds accommodate mostly large and correspondingly valuable luxury boats whose manoeuvring ashore and maintenance would in fact be too much for the owner and crew to cope with. Some of these boats will be large craft whose level of technical equipment will resemble that of a merchant vessel, not to mention the vast dimensions of the surfaces requiring attention (the ship's side, the underwater hull etc). Shed's greatest advantage can be summed up in one sentence: all *you* need do is berth your vessel under the crane in the autumn and fetch it again in the spring.

Naturally, such a complete service represents not only a very convenient option but also an extremely expensive solution to all the problems of laying up. This is a result of the ground rents charged for the sheds, and the workers' rates of pay: a proper boatyard offering the services of all trades – such as hull experts, riggers, electricians, engine specialists, painters, etc – must base its charges on the top rates of pay of well-qualified craftsmen. But, by the same token, there is absolutely nothing for the owner to worry about. Complete service means just that: de-rigging the boat, getting it out of the water, cleaning it, moving it into the shed, propping it up, preparing the engine(s) and all on-board technical equipment (such as batteries, tanks, electrics, hydraulics) for the winter, making good any notified or discovered damage, overhauling the underwater hull come the spring, moving it out of the shed again, getting it into the water, re-rigging it and recommissioning it. And every reputable boatyard will, on top of these many time-consuming jobs, readily take on any additional commissions for modifications, replacements, and checking and maintenance beyond that which is normally done – for an appropriate sum of course! The catalogue of advantages would not be complete if it did not include mention of the fact that these yards are also as a rule accommodating with regard to the timing requirements of their clientele: you can pick your own time for going into winter quarters and coming out. Yard owners cherish good customers – and so they should, they provide their living during the winter months.

However, matters are not quite so simple for those owners who want to winter their craft in a yard shed, but don't want it serviced by the yard. Here we come to the most serious disadvantage of laying up in a yard: many yard owners permit work on laying up boats only by the owner himself and his summer crew/family, but under no circumstances by strangers or – perish the thought – outside experts. There are even a few who will allow nothing of that kind – they expect to get an order for any work needing to be done on the vessel. Since this exceeds the financial capabilities of many owners, the problem often resolves itself by such owners staying away. But as long as there is a shortage of shed berths because there are more and more yachts whose owners like to have them housed over the winter, yard owners can behave in this way. The law of supply and demand applies here also. Where and how you get your boat to pass the winter, aside from other factors, is very much a question of cost.

Deciding on winter quarters

An aid to decision-making, plus cost factors

Having described the various ways in which boats can be laid up, the table on pp. 28–30 gives the full range of criteria as an aid to decision-making. On top of that, we indicate the laying up cost for a medium-sized sailing yacht whose measurements are 11m × 3.4m × 1.8m/8 tonnes. These costs are mean values arrived at through numerous enquiries from clubs, marinas, private premises and boatyards, so individual cases can deviate substantially according to region and overall length – upwards or downwards! Some yards are reluctant to lift the keel of a vertically lifting keel boat, and some charge considerably more for shoring a deep narrow fin keel yacht. If you're not obliged to winter in a certain place, you should obtain quotations from adjoining harbours/undertakings. Where there are several professional yacht-servicing outfits sited together, you can even bargain about laying-up conditions and prices.

The table should help you to find the answer to the following question: Which type of laying up arrangement do you want for your boat? But also, we want to give you some advice that has nothing to do with money or convenience, but instead concerns your familiarity with your vessel: the more you involve yourself in the business of laying up and overhauling your craft, the better you will get to know (and love) it. If a yard has

Action	Club	Marina	Private	Boatyard
De-rig yacht Lift out mast Stow mast and rigging	DIY; poss. use of mast crane £5	Crane hire £10 1 craftsman hour £30	DIY; poss. use of mast crane £10	Crane hire £10 1 craftsman hour £30
Lift yacht out of water High pressure clean for underwater hull Move to winter berth/shed Set up	DIY; poss. use of crane and high pressure cleaner £20	Crane hire £50 Cleaning £10 Transport at cost, say £10	DIY; poss. hire of public crane and high pressure cleaner £20 Transport and crane to barn £10	Crane hire £50 Cleaning £10 Transport £15
Set up yacht on hired cradle	DIY if small yacht	£35	Not customary (own trailer)	Hired cradle £20 excl. deliv.
Set up yacht including building up bilge (blocks and shores)	DIY, wood supplied by club; not for large or deep keeled yachts	£30 to £50 for deep keeled yacht	DIY; usually left on own trailer	£30 to £50 for deep keeled yacht
Cover yacht with own tarpaulin (no frame over)	DIY	0.5 craftsman hours £15	DIY	0.5 craftsman hours £15
Cover yacht with hired tarpaulin (poss. frame over)	Not customary/ DIY	Up to 3 craftsman hours £90 Tarpaulin hire + frame £100	Not customary/ DIY	Up to 3 craftsman hours £90 Tarpaulin hire £50

Action	Club	Marina	Private	Boatyard
Prepare on-board technical equipment for winter	DIY	Up to 3 craftsman hours £90	DIY	Frame £50 Up to 3 craftsman hours £90
Engine	Materials (oil, filters, seals) £30	Materials £30	Materials £30	Materials (oil, filters, seals) £30
Remove and charge batteries Reinstall batteries in spring	DIY	Charging; lump sum £10	DIY (often no power supply)	Charge; lump sum £15
Rent, open berth 11 × 3.4 = 40m² for 5 months	£50	18.–/m² £500	10.–/m² £300	25.–/m² £600
Rent, shed 11 × 3.4 = 40m² for 5 months	£150	43.–/m² £700	18.–/m² £400	50.–/m² £900
Sand and repaint underwater hull	DIY; paint £50	Up to 6 craftsman hours £180. Paint £50	DIY; paint £50	Up to 6 craftsman hours £180. Paint £50
Remove tarpaulin Move to crane Relaunch yacht	DIY; fee for crane £10	0.5 craftsman hours £15 Crane hire £50	DIY; Transport from barn- crane £10 Hire public harbour crane £30	0.5 craftsman hours £15 Transport £15 Crane hire £50

Action	Club	Marina	Private	Boatyard
Re-rig yacht Replace mast	DIY Poss. use of mast crane £5	2 craftsman hours £60 Poss. use of mast crane £10	DIY Poss. use of mast crane £10	2 craftsman hours £60 Crane hire £10
Recommission yacht and on-board technical equipment	DIY	Poss. 2 craftsman hours £60	DIY	Poss. 2 craftsman hours £60
Maximum cost (shed berth)	£270	£1655	£570	£1865
Maximum cost (berth in open)	£170	£1455	£470	£1565

carried out repairs to your boat, it is sometimes hard to be certain that the job has been done well. If you want to be absolutely sure that your knowledge of your boat and the technical equipment on board is accurate, you have to lend a hand yourself. Of course, that requires time, tools and expertise. It is this expertise that this book is intended to provide. We shall describe all procedures and jobs in such a way that you have the know-how to carry them out yourself – without having to depend on the expensive services of professionals.

Preparations while still afloat

Before the boat is finally hanging from the crane there are lots of jobs to be done, either because they *have* to be completed while it is still in the water or because it's simpler to do them then. De-rigging and lifting out the mast can be done ashore or in the water; preparing the technical equipment on board (in particular the auxiliary engine) for winter and thoroughly cleaning the deck and superstructure are easier to carry out while the vessel is still afloat.

Dealing with sails and rigging

Cleaning, drying and storing the sails

Doing it yourself

The sails are one of the highly stressed parts of a yacht. During the sailing season they are exposed to rain, grime, salt water and sunshine; they flap in the wind and chafe against the rigging. They have to be cleaned, dried carefully, and checked for damage before stowing away, because salt-soaked sails never dry and corrosive grime (eg from the smokestacks of merchant shipping) gnaws at the sailcloth during the long winter.

With the DIY method, cleaning has to be restricted to rinsing with fresh water. To do this, the sails are hoisted before being removed and a powerful jet from a hose is directed at them from both sides – a wet business, which furthermore requires a dry and sunny day with a slight breeze. The hoisted sails are then left to dry in the wind, care being taken to see that they don't shake too much or beat against the mast or the rigging (haul in the mainsheet, belay the genoa sheet).

If you have enough room and a strong clothes-line in your own garden, you can of course clean the sails there. Spread them out on the lawn and spray-wash well (possibly additionally going over them with a scrubber and a weak soap solution, and spray-rinsing them afterwards), then hang them from the clothes-line so that they can swing freely to dry. But there is a hazard with this lawn-method: blades of freshly cut grass are very difficult to remove from sailcloth! For the owners of smallish boats there is a third method of getting salt-soaked and dirty sails clean. Sails up to about 20 square metres in area can be soaked in the bath in warm soapy water then rinsed in clean water. However, the disadvantage is that they have to be carried – dripping all the way – through the house out to the clothes-line.

After cleaning and drying comes a painstaking inspection for damage: every one of the seams, every eyelet, every slide, and the trimming lines in the leech have to be checked carefully for loose threads, signs of chafing and breakage. The batten pockets, luff and foot, merit special attention, whether the sail has a luffline running in a mast groove or sliders. If a sail has to go to the sailmaker, then take it in the autumn. For many sailmakers, October to December is their slack period; they have time to do repairs and are often prepared to give discounts.

Finally, all sails are expertly folded – namely, folded cloth-breadth on cloth-breadth (in the case of the mainsail, starting at the foot). When folded a couple of times, they will go into their sail bag and be ready to spend the winter in some dry and airy spot (eg your loft). Incidentally, the ever more popular in-mast reefing sails should be dealt with in exactly the same way. Preferably, they should not be left rolled up in the mast, unless the mast is stored in a dry shed.

Using professionals

If you think that doing this job yourself will be too time-consuming and laborious, there is an alternative that is much simpler – though not exactly cheap. There are many places where sailmakers have recognized a market-opening for valet-ting and are offering their clients a complete service. This consists of proper laundering of the sails in industrial washing machines (highly effective – the sails become really white again) followed by drying in hot-air driers. The sailmaker then checks the sails carefully for damage, which he makes good straight away. Finally, he stores them correctly until the following season. All you need do yourself is remove the sails, put them into their bags, and deliver them to the sailmaker's shop. From then on, you can safely forget all about them. This privilege has to be paid for of course: on average, sailmakers charge £2–3 per square metre of sail area just for washing, drying, checking and storing. The outfit of sails for our specimen 11 metre yacht (3 genoas, 2 jibs, 1 mainsail, 1 spinnaker = c.200 square metres) can thus cost some £400–600 for cleaning and storage.

De-rigging – preparatory work in the berth

The amount of time a yacht can spend under the mast crane for dropping the mast is usually fairly limited: either other owners who are waiting pressurize you, or you have to pay on a time basis. So since only a short time can be allowed for this job, some preparatory work has to be done while you are still in the berth. The following tasks need to be carried out:

1 Remove the sails;
2 Dismantle the mainsheet;
3 Dismantle the main boom kicking strap;
4 Strip the main boom (reefing pendants, tensioner, etc);
5 Detach the topping lift from the boom;
6 Take down the main boom and remove from on board;
7 Take down the spinnaker boom and remove from on board;
8 Lash all the halyards and flag lines to the mast;
9 Possibly unreeve the roller reefing lines; lash to the mast/forestay;
10 *Mast electrics* pull out all the plugs, lash to the mast; and screw up the sockets;
11 Undo the aerial connections (backstay);
12 'Unlock' all the rigging screws (take out split pins, remove tape bandages, etc);

13 *Masthead rig* disconnect the deck ends of all the lower shrouds, second standing backstay, second forestay and lash securely to the mast;

14 *7/8 rig* disconnect the deck ends of the after lower shrouds, running backstays, possibly second standing back-/forestay; and lash securely to the mast;

15 *Tabernacle mast* undo the nut of the mast bolt;

16 *Stepped mast* remove the mast collar, and any cladding below deck;

17 *Any shrouds/stays still standing* slack back the rigging screws to 'hand tight';

18 Undo/free all other screwed connections (shackles, bolts etc);

19 Prepare the slings for dropping the mast;

20 Lay out the tools (hammer, universal pliers, marline spike) ready to hand;

21 Prepare the trestle/stowage for stowing the mast on the deck if relevant;

22 Position the truck for the mast conveniently if relevant;

23 Assemble the helpers;

24 Agree the crane hire.

Once all this preparatory work has been done, the yacht is ready to be towed under the mast crane and no further time there is required than that taken to drop the mast.

Moving to the crane and dropping the mast

More so than when a yacht is going alongside a jetty 'normally', two things are important when making fast underneath the mast crane: the mast of the yacht must be as precisely as possible under the jib of the mast crane in its swung-out position, and the yacht must not move either lengthways or sideways while the mast is being dropped. So, lay out enough fenders on the side towards the jetty, and use bow and stern lines as well as springs to moor the boat securely.

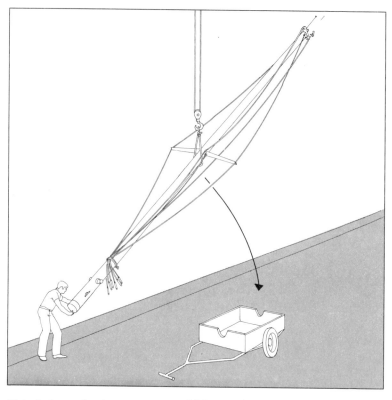

This is how the 'asparagus-stalk' hangs from the mast crane.
The rope sling should bear against the spreaders, but outside
the fittings for the lower shrouds. All shrouds and stays are
carefully lashed to the mast before laying it down or re-
stepping it. One person guides the mast foot by hand –
particularly if the mast is top-heavy.

Another thing to watch for is that the masthead (with its
delicate wind-sensing electronics, burgee staff, etc) does not
collide with the crane's jib when the mast is being lifted: it may
be that the crane has to lift the mast at a bit of an angle to
keep the masthead clear. But if that is so, it is even more
important that the warps don't allow the boat to move.

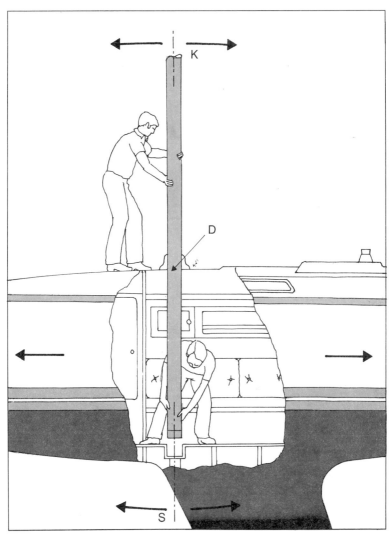

Stepping or dropping a mast on the keelson is a bit more difficult. Since the mast has a fixed pivot point in the aperture D through the deck, either the crane jib K or the vessel S has to be moved lengthways to get the heel of the mast into or out of the step.

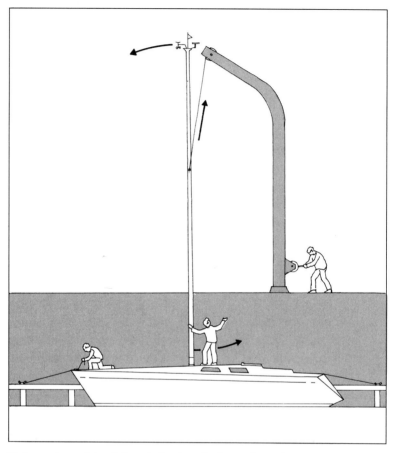

If there is a risk of the delicate wind-sensing electronics, the aerial or the burgee staff colliding with the crane jib, the crane sling must pull on the mast at an angle. In this situation the boat must definitely not move astern, and the foot of the mast must be guided carefully.

Dropping stepped masts extending through the cabin roof right down to the keel often presents special difficulties. They either have to be lifted absolutely vertically, or helpers on deck have to veer and haul guide ropes as necessary to ensure that even where the pull is at an angle the mast hangs vertically again as soon as the head is clear of the crane.

To drop a mast (although many boatyards will not allow an owner to de-rig the boat themselves) you normally use a rope sling which the crane hook pulls up against the spreader. The sling (made with a bowline) must have an eye large enough to clear the mast-head lamp, spinnaker fittings or anything else that might get in the way. It is laid around the shrouds/stays already lashed to the mast and should bear directly against the spreader mountings close to the mast, not against the lower-shroud terminals or fittings.

As soon as the crane has pulled the sling into the right position and is taking some of the load, the shrouds and stays still standing can be undone. There are several ways of going about this: some owners unscrew the rigging screws and leave the sleeves of these on the chain-plates, but a better method is to release the entire screws by removing the bolt through the deck-end and storing them with the rigging. That leaves the deck clear (and eliminates the risk of stumbling on the boat while it is in winter quarters), and makes it easier to clean it and check the chain-plates.

The released shrouds and stays are now also carefully lashed to the mast to prevent them damaging the deck and the super-structure, then the mast is finally lifted clear of the craft. This requires three helpers: one operates the crane, a second guides the heel ashore from the deck (a warning: there are top-heavy masts whose heel has to have a line fastened to it before lifting starts), and the third takes charge once the mast is ashore, lowering it on to a truck for transport.

If you do not intend to store the mast ashore, but instead to keep it on deck – as a ridge piece for the laying up tarpaulin or to go with the yacht for laying up elsewhere – appropriate supporting and securing arrangements have to be made ready, and possibly more rigging removed.

Stowing the mast on deck

Yacht masts are almost always of such a length that they project beyond the bow and the stern. For this reason, the main burden of the laid down rig can often be borne by the pushpit and the pulpit, their height increased by additional supports if necessary because of the height of the superstructure. Many owners construct such supports for themselves using squared timber, to be used again in future winters. In addition to the support fore and aft, the mast should have a couple of supports part-way along to stop it sagging. And of course it has to be lashed to stop it moving sideways. If it is to serve as ridge piece for a laying-up tarpaulin, you first have to do some more unrigging:

If the mast is to be stowed on deck, either to be taken to the winter quarters with the boat or to act as a ridge-piece for the tarpaulin, I recommend a sturdy support fitted on top of the pushpit and the pulpit. To prevent sagging, this mast is additionally supported amidships by a horse or notched beam (see also the diagrams on pp. 41 and 42).

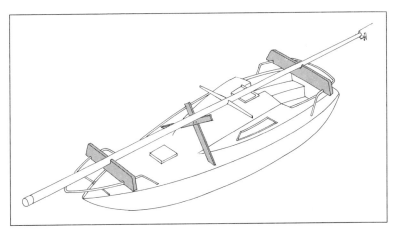

This diagram illustrates the way the mast rests securely on two wooden structures accurately fitting the pushpit and pulpit. Additionally, a horse supports the mast amidships. It must also of course have lashings to stop it moving lengthways or sideways.

fittings and equipment that get in the way, such as the steaming light, any spinnaker fittings and the spreaders, have to be taken down.

If all you're doing with the mast on deck is transporting it further by sea or on inland waterways, don't forget to fit a steaming lamp above deck level to comply with the regulations.

Storing the mast ashore; checking the rigging

Many a marina and a lot of clubs require their customers/members to remove more or less all of the rigging from the mast, to save stowage space. At the very least, that means removing or folding in the awkward spreaders to make handling easier.

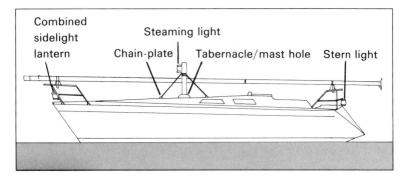

Steaming light on a yacht with the mast dropped. If she is proceeding to winter quarters under own power with the mast dropped, a steaming light must be rigged on deck at dusk. It has to be rigged 1 metre higher than the sidelights. It can be mounted on a squared baulk of timber set up alongside the tabernacle or mast hole and stayed to the lower-shroud chain-plates.

This may be laborious, but has its advantages: a mast free of shrouds, stays, spreaders and lamps is much easier to clean – something that should be done before stowing it away for the winter because it has acquired salt and grime. And also a thorough inspection of the rigging leaves you with peace of mind: are all pins and safety rings in good condition; are mast fittings riveted, and screwed connections free from cracks; the shrouds free from broken wires; the halyard sheaves turning freely; all electric leads and the wind-sensing electronics in good order? Incidentally, before taking them down I recommend fitting inscribed (eg pt-ls-a: port lower shroud aft) strips of adhesive tape to the individual rigging wires, to avoid any problems when re-rigging in the spring. Finally, roll up all rigging wires separately and stow them in a dry place.

Before stowing it away, you need to clean and check the whole mast. In the case of wooden masts, now becoming rare, this involves a thorough wash followed by a check for black spots and rot, followed by immediate treatment of any damage that you find. Aluminium masts are cleaned and protected in one process using a special polish for anodized aluminium obtainable from chandleries, builders' merchants, or directly from the manufacturers of aluminium windows.

Whether you supplement this by wrapping your mast in a protective envelope of plastic sheet or old bed sheets is a matter for you to decide. At any rate, it is ready – de-rigged, checked, cleaned and attended to – for its winter stowage. It should be stored in as dry a place as possible and supported in several places against sagging. When stowing the mast, take care that it is not in direct contact with ferrous supports – small pieces of wooden board placed in between will prevent corrosion.

Preparing technical equipment for winter

Preparing the engine

The cooling system

One of the jobs best carried out while the craft is still in its berth is maintenance and preservation of the cooling circuit of our water-cooled engines. I scarcely need to remind you that there are two versions of these: directly cooled ones with sea water flowing through all the pipes, the pump and the engine cooling passages; and indirectly cooled ones with a primary cooling circuit permanently filled with fresh water conveying its waste heat to a second, salt water, circuit. Although the engine with direct sea-water cooling require greater care, those with two-circuit cooling still have to have at least the one with sea water dealt with. In both cases, it is a matter of getting rid of the corrosive (salt-)sea water from the cooling circuit and also, as far as possible, removing deposits such as salt crystals, scale, rust, algal material and strands of seaweed.

Next the cooling system has to be protected by special anticor-rosive agents to prevent rusting while it is exposed to air over the winter. Since this job is of the greater importance in the case of directly cooled engines, here is a checklist:

1 Close the cooling water inlet sea cock.
2 Disconnect the supply hose at the sea cock, the filter or the pump. Introduce fresh water by hose from the jetty (better with a container in between so that the engine itself draws in the fresh water).
3 Start the engine, let it warm up – possibly under load by clutching in the prop – and let it run for at least an hour.
4 Stop the engine. Open the sea-water filter, clean the strainers and reassemble.
5 Preservation of the cooling system by the introduction of anticorrosive oil (Esso make a range of specialized marine oils with anticorrosion inhibitors, called Blue Riband marine oils) or antifreeze:
   – with anticorrosive oil: fill the container with oil/water emulsion (eg 1:20; 1 litre oil to 20 litres water), start the engine and let it empty the container, catching the emulsion in the basin at the exhaust outlet and disposing of it appropriately. Drain the rest of the emulsion from the engine by opening the drain cocks on the cylinder block (one per cylinder and one on the water collector before the exhaust), because there is no antifreeze in the emulsion;
   – with antifreeze: fill the container with antifreeze/fresh water (eg 1:5, 1 litre antifreeze to 5 litres water), start the engine and let it empty the container. The antifreeze remains in the engine.
6 Reconnect the sea-water hose to the sea cock.
7 Take out the cooling water pump impeller (but not if using antifreeze), check it and store it separately.
8 Drain any water heaters/heat exchangers.

If in addition to the work described above, intensive cleaning of the cooling circuit is needed; because deposits are beginning to choke the narrower coolant passages in the engine block and thus creating cooling problems, we recommend acid cleaning of the system with up to 50 per cent strength acetic acid or with

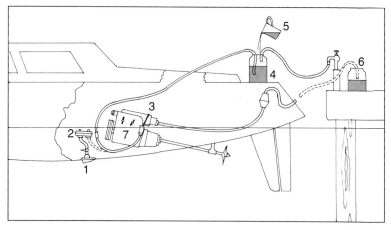

Washing through and preserving a single-circuit (sea-water) cooling system with fresh water from tap on the jetty.
1 Sea cock. 2 Sea-water filter. 3 Cooling water pump. 4 Intermediate container. 5 Preservative oil. 6 Recovery container. 7 Cooling water drain cocks.

If the engine is only to be washed through, then 5 and 6 are omitted. Instead, the circuit is filled with antifreeze which remains in the engine.

radiator flush. Even fresh water may be sufficient.

This is how you do it. Remove the thermostat and create a closed circuit as follows:

- Fill the container with the fluid to be used.
- Connect a suction hose from the container to the engine and dip it into the container.
- Return the cooling water from the 'after' engine to the container, by means of a hose fixed to the exhaust outlet.
- Keep an eye on the cooling water thermometer: the engine should heat up until it gets to the red zone because cleaning is then most effective, but don't let it overheat!
- Wear gloves because the cleaning fluid harms the skin.
- Dispose of the cleaning fluid appropriately.

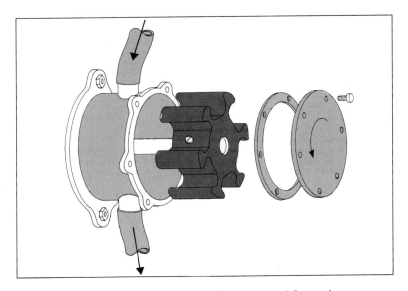

Water pump impeller. This should be removed from the pump during laying up. Usually it and its shaft can be extracted from the casing by hand. Before replacing it, the blades of the impeller (which is made of a special rubber) are inspected for cracks. The pump cover should be fitted with a new gasket.

The engine cooling circuit is now protected against frost and corrosion and, in so far as this was necessary, has been freed from deposits, etc. The same work, or at least parts of it, should be undertaken on engines with two-circuit cooling. The internal, fresh-water, circuit should be checked to see that it is frost-proof, antifreeze as required for winter temperatures being added if necessary; the sea-water circuit should be washed through and preserved.

The lube oil system
Engine oil that has seen a whole sailing season's service not only looks pitch-black because it contains soot in suspension from the

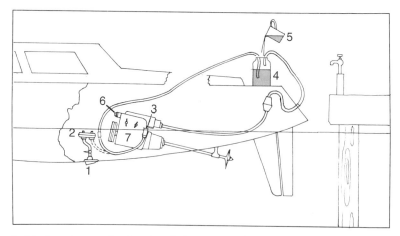

Acid cleaning a single-circuit (sea-water) cooling system with a special cleaning agent or dilute acetic acid.

1 Sea cock. 2 Sea-water filter. 3 Cooling water pump.
4 Container with fresh water. 5 Cleaning fluid. 6 Thermostat.
7 Cooling water drain cocks.

In the closed circuit thus created, the mixture of water and cleaning fluid heats up quickly. So keep an eye on the cooling water thermometer. After the dirty cleaning fluid has been appropriately disposed of, the engine must be washed through thoroughly again with fresh water.

diesel fuel burnt in the engine, but also because it contains materials such as sulphur, dissolved hydrocarbons and perhaps water which, during the winter, attack the lubricated surfaces sensitive to them (particularly bearings, cylinder walls). So the oil and filter change that must be due anyway should be carried out in the autumn. This is a convenient opportunity, because the engine has been brought to running temperature in the course of the cooling-system preservation. The best time is after item 3 (see section on p. 45). At that point you can:

1 Drain as much of the old oil out of the engine as possible by
   removing the drain plug. (cont. on p. 50)

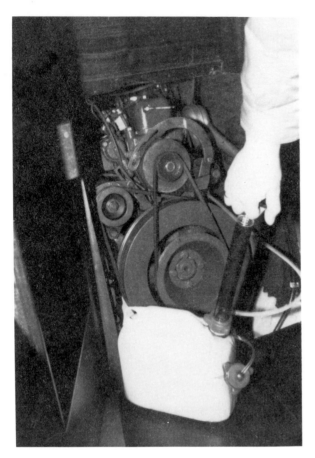

There is no mess if you use this can for the oil change. The hand pump screwed on to it draws a vacuum in the can; the dirty oil is drawn in without any splashes.

2 Change the oil filter cartridge.
3 Refill with fresh oil to the upper mark on the dipstick.
4 Restart the engine and let it run for a few minutes.

If you want to be extra kind to your engine, you should also wash through the lubricating system – you will be amazed at how black the rinsing oil coming out of the engine is. This you do after item 1 above, as follows:

- After drawing off the old oil (don't change the filter cartridge yet), fill the sump up to the lower mark on the dipstick with (cheap) supermarket oil, eg HD SAE 20 single grade or HDX Essolube API CC/FF.
- Run the engine for 15 mins.
- Draw off the rinsing oil.
- Change the oil filter cartridge.
- Refill with fresh oil to the upper mark on the dipstick.
- Restart the engine and let it run for a few minutes.

Finally, it is worth while additionally protecting the cylinders against corrosion by removing the filter from the air intake and – either with the engine running or with it stopped and the inlet valves open – spraying in protective oil (eg MoS_2-oil or gun oil like SPINESSO 10).

And don't forget the reversing gear, should that be due for an oil change at this time. All that this needs is a change of oil; no washing through or other protective measures are required.

Fuel system
Diesel fuel, not to mention petrol, does not as a rule contain any anticorrosive additives, but it does contain dirt and water, even if only in very small quantities. For that reason, the fuel system also should undergo a preservation process for the long winter months ahead, to protect the tank, pipelines, injection pump and injection nozzles (carburettor, in the case of a petrol engine).

With diesel engines – the most frequently encountered type – the following is involved:

1 Prepare a small (1–2 litre) container with a 1:5 mixture of anticorrosive oil (eg Esso IL 1838) and diesel fuel.

2 *Fuel prefilter*: drain off the water from the separator; change the filter cartridge.

3 *Fine filter*: empty the casing and wipe with a dry cloth; change the cartridge.

4 Break into the pipeline between the tank and prefilter and (possibly using an extension hose) let the end hang into the container.

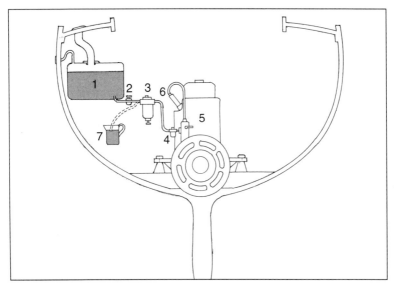

Preservation of a diesel engine fuel system.
1 Fuel tank with filling and vent pipe. 2 Shut-off cock.
3 Prefilter with water separator (drainhole with bolt at bottom).
4 Fine filter. 5 Injection pump with manual operating lever.
6 Injection nozzle. 7 Container with fuel/anticorrosive oil mixture.

Following preservation, the fuel system must be carefully freed from air, by opening the vent screws on the fine filter, the prefilter, and the injection pump and, at the same time, operating the pump manual lever.

5 Vent the fuel system using the hand pump on the injection pump.
6 Start the engine and let it run for 5–10 mins.
7 Reconnect the fuel line to the tank.
8 Vent the fuel system once again.
9 Fill the tank to the brim as protection against condensation and to reduce the risk of explosion.

The work described here is very extensive and laborious, but it is certainly effective – and indeed what many engine manufacturers recommend in their operating instructions. The continuous use of a fuel additive such as Esso IL 1838 substantially simplifies the preparation of the fuel system for winter, eliminating the need to disconnect the fuel line and the repeated venting.

A final job that may be undertaken after preserving the fuel system – although perhaps not every year – is cleaning the air filter (washing through with paraffin followed by impregnating the filter gauze with oil or changing the paper cartridge). Lastly, the injection nozzles should not be forgotten. If you remove them in the autumn, have them checked (pressure test, expert assessment of spray cone quality, setting of correct pressure value) by diesel specialists and fit them again at once; in the subsequent season you will have the pleasure of having a diesel engine in your boat that starts easily, doesn't smoke and uses less fuel.

Protection against external corrosion
Rusty boat engines not only look bad, they also deteriorate more quickly – but this time from the outside inwards. So it's not a bad idea, on completion of the preservation work on the cooling, lube oil and fuel systems, to spray the engine and the whole bilge in its compartment with a so-called cold-cleansing fluid, leaving it to act for a quarter of an hour and then hosing everything down with fresh water. If you do this while the engine is still warm, everything will soon be dry again; now is the time to repair damage to enamel/paint and the engine can

subsequently be lightly sprayed with anticorrosive oil (eg MoS_2 oil or Esso IL 1838).

Preparing the electrics

Our first concern must be the batteries for starting the engine and for generating light. They must be topped up with distilled water, cleaned on the outside, and either continuously connected to a charger or recharged fully about every four weeks – on board, if that is permitted. This is because lead-acid batteries discharge by themselves, even if no current is being taken off; they are only safe from frost when fully charged. Since charging releases so-called detonating gas, many laying-up site operators require batteries to be removed from the boatshed.

Also, all other batteries that could leak or burst need to be removed from clocks, flashlights, flashing distress beacons, radios and similar equipment. Most owners will decide to take home their delicate on-board electronics – maritime-radio sets, radios, navigational computers and echosounders. However, those gadgets that use electricity – such as navigation lights, pumps, generators, electric motors (steering gear, winches), and particularly all exposed plug sockets – should if possible be protected by spraying with anticorrosive oil (eg MoS_2 oil or Esso IL 1838); this will keep out the moisture. A minor but effective trick is to mask all electric switches; that prevents their contact surfaces corroding even over a lengthy laying-up period.

Preparing the tanks, pipelines, WC, fire extinguishers, liferaft, winches, wheel steering gear, engine controls

Before laying up the boat, indeed while it is still in the water, you must empty the drinking water tank and, if you have one,

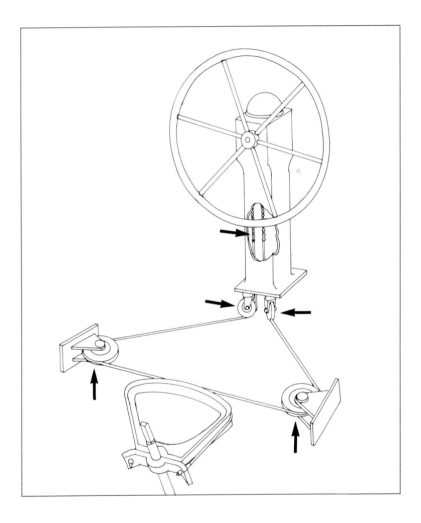

Wheel steering gear using ropes has to have the control chain in the pedestal and the guide-pulleys of the ropes greased regularly. Before laying up is a good time to do this.

the holding tank of the on-board toilet, to avoid the risk of frost damage and fungal growth. It's also a good idea to clean the tanks, either by washing out by hand through the inspection hole or at least by a thorough flush-through with a lot of fresh water.

Fresh-water pipelines are usually very difficult to empty; the best technique is to blow them through with the tank empty and the taps open. Lines that just can't be emptied completely (toilet pump) are protected against frost by pouring in a beaker of undiluted antifreeze.

All equipment not especially sensitive to low temperature but sensitive to humidity should be removed from on board for the winter: automatically inflating life jackets, distress flares, fire extinguishers, and the liferaft if carried. For these, the same thing is valid as for sails: anything needing maintenance, overhaul or repair should now be handed over to the experts.

Since all of these jobs will require the use of tools, cleaning materials and lubricants, how about at the same time devoting some attention to your sheet and halyard winches, the (wheel) steering gear, and the engine controls? Often, these are treated in a cavalier fashion. The winches should be dismantled as far as possible; the parts (gearwheels, roller bearings, ratchets, springs) need thorough cleaning using paraffin, and then thorough greasing with special winch grease.

Wheel steering gear has to have the control chain inside the pedestal and the guide-pulleys for the ropes greased or, if it has rod gearing, the gearwheels and bearings.

Engine gear change and accelerator operation is usually by cables, which get a few drops of clean engine oil dripped into the top end. That usually means taking off the lid/casing cover of the single-lever control to get at the cables. Any other lubricating points of the controls also would appreciate a drop of oil or a dab of grease – which is combined with a check of any split pins, screwed connections and locknuts.

Finally, you close the sea cocks and, if possible, pour some antifreeze into the pipes/hoses leading to them. Having done all this, the technical equipment on board can no longer come to any harm and will survive the long winter safely. You can then be fairly confident that the mechanical gear will be ready to resume functioning in the spring.

Cleaning the deck, superstructure and bilges

You simply can't stress it enough: corrosive deposits of salt and grime, which can be brought on board just as easily by the air as by sea or river water, must be thoroughly removed before leaving the boat for the winter. Because salt is notoriously hygroscopic and keeps on extracting moisture from the air, a salt-encrusted boat never dries properly. And airborne grime – mostly acidic – turns every surface (whether varnish, paint, gel coat or metal) dull and porous over the course of the winter.

Thus, a thorough wash-down for deck and superstructure (the hull gets its turn when ashore) while still in the summer berth and before laying up is absolutely essential. Most skippers are fussy about cleanliness anyway. Just about every single one has his own method and swears by a particular washing agent or detergent. There's certainly no harm in that, provided two basic principles are always observed. The first is that washing agents should be alkaline so that they chemically neutralize acidic grime; they should also be superfatting. They should be substantially biodegradable, because they will ultimately end up in the harbour. In fact, the less sophisticated the chemistry the better: the good old soft soap is man enough to deal with just about every kind of grime, whether it's on GRP, wood or metal. The second principle is this: any mechanical aids used, such as brushes, scrubbers or sponges, must not scratch, scour or abrade. So it's best to use soft, natural-bristle brushes, soft sponges and, above all, a lot of fresh water. Under no circumstances should gel coat be cleaned using plastic scrubbers like the household sponges or pot scourers found in the kitchen. Plastic they may be, but they still scratch shiny surfaces. Stubborn dirt may be removed with solvent-based 'boat cleaner', provided a sealing layer of wax is applied subsequently to avoid bare gel coat chalking and becoming dull. Recently, high-pressure cleaning jets, which 'blow away' everything not firmly fastened to the boat by means of a fine-water spray under enormous pressure (up to 120 bar), have been gaining in popularity. 'Everything', though, is just that: as well as all the dirt, window seals, rubber parts of plugs/sockets and electric leads, loose lids, hoods over fan inlets/outlets and covers such as those over the engine instruments will also be blown away. Teak-laid decks get particularly short shrift: the softer parts of the wood can be gouged out, leaving only the harder part of the graining. Given this treatment regularly two or three times a year, you will have a deck that's always as clean as a whistle, but you'll also be needing a new one within a few years. So if it has to be the high-pressure jet for convenience, then pick one that can be throttled down to a gentle 40–60 bar. Also, use it at an acute angle and from a distance of at least 30 centimetres from the target.

Whichever way you go about it, once you've finished this job, your boat should be really clean above deck, particularly the parts normally out of sight – such as under the cockpit gratings.

Finally, when all the washing water has run off, it's the turn of the bilges (and the chain locker and cockpit locker seats) which probably now have quite a bit more water in them than before the big wash. Before pumping the bilges out into the harbour, any diesel fuel or lubricating oil (from preparing the engine for winter?) in the dirty brew should be removed. This is quite simple really, using one of the oil/water separating agents produced by various firms and available in powder, cloth and sponge form. Simplest of all to use are sponges: they suck up only the oil; they are ready for re-use after squeezing out into an old bucket; and they leave the water in the bilges clean enough to go back over the side where it belongs.

Should you be unable to get all the water out because a bilge is very deep, a shot of antifreeze safeguards the lowest portion of the boat against a (dangerous) solid block of ice.

Getting the boat ashore

The point at which a boat leaves the water represents a potential hazard; whereas a moment ago its hull was still supported over its whole surface and steadied in stable equilibrium by the water around it, its weight is now – augmented by the mass of the displaced body of water no longer there – concentrated on just a few points. In the past, accidents, serious damage and even total losses during hoisting out and relaunching of vessels were pretty frequent, but nowadays modern crane and transport systems have made such undertakings almost child's play.

Slipping

Today, slips where boats are brought ashore on trucks running on rails or a sloping surface are a rarity – found sometimes in long-established, traditional sailing clubs. For this operation, the truck on its cable is run down into the harbour far enough for the boat to be floating with its keel over the truck framework. The craft has then to be 'floated in' very precisely between the four to six stanchions, so that the keel settles on to the middle of the truck and the gap between the stanchions and the hull is the same all round. The vessel is now secured to the stanchions and the truck winched in until the keel is resting over its full length on the truck's central beam. Fenders are then placed between hull and stanchions, the latter being at the same time adjusted from on deck to match the hull shape. As the truck is winched in further, the weight of the boat comes to rest entirely on the keel and it leans against the stanchions on one side or the other. The procedure is tedious, manpower-intensive and, in the event of inexpert or careless handling, is potentially risky. Furthermore, it is nowadays really only suitable for the traditional type of boat with a long keel; modern fin-keel boats' stability on the truck is precarious, they tend to tilt back on to their stern on the sloping slipway, or else it may be altogether impossible to slip them because of the shape of the lower edge of the keel.

Indeed, the whole installation continually causes the operators a great deal of worry. It may be for instance that the rails become sanded up and have to be flushed clean under water before slipping can start, or the truck may become derailed, or the installation may be seriously damaged by the movement of ice in the winter.

Craning out

All yards and marinas, and many clubs, nowadays use cranes for hoisting boats out of the water and lowering them in again. However, the general designation 'crane' covers a whole assortment of technical equipment, all with advantages and disadvantages. It ranges from the simplest stationary trestle crane, even derrick, through stationary pillar cranes with fixed jibs and various stationary and wheeled slewing cranes with luffing jibs, to mobile cranes and, finally, there is the latest and most expensive of the devices – the travelhoist or travelift. One of the criteria in the acquisition of cranes is obviously the price: it

The simplest and cheapest solution to the crane problem: a derrick. The most expensive component is the electric winch with remote control via a wandering lead.

ranges from about £10,000 to buy a simple slewing derrick with a 10 tonne electric winch up to about £150,000 for an ultra-modern travelhoist with all-wheel steering, four hoisting winches and a lifting capacity of 70 tonnes – this includes the lifting slings which alone swallow up £2000–3000. You have to add to this the substantial cost of the special quay installation on whose parallel tracks the travelift runs to straddle the boat to be hoisted.

Alongside the purchase of cranes, against which a low level of use over the year usually has to be set, a standard practice

Out of the water and over to winter quarters in one go: the travelhoist is the ideal device for transporting yachts ashore safely and rapidly with minimum manpower. The stress on the hull is kept low by the favourable angle of the slings.

By virtue of its low overall height, this wheeled transporter with special equipment can drive right into the shed with the boat.

A slewing pillar crane with traverses and lifting girth. The limited reach restricts its capability to lifting yachts ashore and setting them down on transport vehicles.

Many clubs employ mobile cranes for hoisting boats out of the water and moving them about on land – a cheap solution because a skipper pays only the rent.

is the hiring of mobile cranes for only a few days, perhaps even hours, at the beginning and end of the season. The hourly rate – travelling time must of course be included – for a modern self-propelled crane with a 10 tonne lifting capacity at a reach of 15 metres and capable of travelling with this load currently averages £20 to £90 per hour including travelling time. Some firms impose a minimum period of hire – sometimes a full day. VAT will probably be charged as well, but you may be able to negotiate a reduction for cash in hand in some areas!

Some boatyard owners will not allow a crane hired by a boatowner to operate from their premises without inflicting a charge. Neither will many allow a transport firm collecting a boat to use its own lifting gear if the yard possesses its own crane. The owner would do well to establish what a yard will and will not permit.

A second criterion in deciding on some specific crane system concerns what is demanded from it over all. If all it needs to do is hoist boats out of the water and set them down on a trailer, boat carriage or cradle located within the (fixed) reach of the crane, then the simplest form of derrick will do. If, on the other hand, the vessel is to be craned out and taken to its winter quarters without transfer, then a mobile crane is needed for open-air berths; for a berth in a shed, a travelift is best.

It's also a question of manpower requirements. Using a modern lift, two people can hoist vessels of any size, transport them, and set them down on their stand accurately to the nearest centimetre.

Crane gear

The pad eye

In the past, when there were no artificial-fibre lifting slings, no mobile cranes and no travelifts, yacht and boat builders endowed their craft with a 'pad eye'. This is a massive threaded bolt with an eye, which was screwed into the keel inside the hull precisely in the boat's centre of gravity. A stout wire rope – a lifting-strop – was shackled to this eye and taken vertically up on deck through the cabin roof via a specially provided opening with a screwed lid. A crane hoisted the boat out of the water hanging from this strop.

Nowadays, this sort of equipment is found only in isolated cases, on older boats. However, it has its advantages: no slings that locally stress the hull/gall the (varnished?) outside surface, nor can they slip and damage the rudder/prop/log/echosounder; and the boat hangs, as it is designed to do, suspended from the centre of gravity (CG) at the keel (ie where the bracing is strongest). Naturally, this sort of equipment has to be looked after carefully; where you have several tonnes of boat 'hanging from a single thread' as it were, you can't afford any broken wires in individual strands, rust or damaged threads. And care is needed during the hoisting: the strop has to be properly cushioned where it passes through the cabin roof because the boat tends to 'lean against' it as it swings on the crane.

Frame and slings

The use of artificial-fibre fabric lifting slings has for a long time been established practice wherever boats are hoisted by crane. They adapt to the shape of the hull above and below the waterline, have a reasonably large bearing surface, and are easily handled even by non-experts. Nevertheless, they stress the hull significantly and in an unnatural fashion, and may even damage the craft.

The stressing of a vessel's hull by lifting it with slings takes two forms. On the one hand, the slings act athwartships as though they wanted to squash the hull; on the other, the hull bends lengthways – something clearly visible in the case of many a lightly built modern vessel. Both forms have to be minimized, by having the slings leading upwards from the hull at least vertically and lying as close as possible to the boat's centre of gravity (ie near the keel). So, as a matter of principle, a

This is how the boat hangs from the crane. The rectangular frame sees to it that the slings are in the right place and at the right angle. But the prop shaft is in danger: markings on deck must ensure that the sling does not inadvertently bear too far aft and damage the shaft.

rectangular or square frame is used: fitting between crane cable and hull, it ensures correct spacing and lead of the slings.

Special care has to be taken when floating the boat into the slings which either hang down into the water in a bight or, having been detached from the frame at one end, are pulled through under the hull. Now, and later when hoisting, the prop shaft and A-bracket, the prop, the log impeller, and possibly the transducer of the echosounder are in danger! If you don't know precisely where along the hull the slings have to be at deck level so as not to cause any costly damage below the waterline, take the opportunity of this laying up to stick some coloured adhesive tape to the toerail as unobtrusive markings for next time.

Once the slings are in the right place, they should additionally be roped together lengthways to stop them sliding fore and aft on the slippery surface of the underwater hull. Again, before hoisting, you pass ashore the ends of lines secured fore and aft on deck; that allows two helpers to steady the boat against possible wind pressure and turn it into the right position relative to the boat trolley or cradle.

Slings under the travelift

Everything that has already been said of course applies here also, but with some simplification. Travelifts don't require a special traverse because by virtue of their frame construction they lead the slings correctly anyway – indeed, mostly in the form of an opened-up 'U', which reduces the hull stress still further. Floating into the slings is simple too because it is the lift that runs, with the slings right down in the water, over the boat which is lying centrally between the tracks of the lift basin. The need for fore and aft lines also disappears, because the hull has little room to swing between the four legs of the travelift.

Another major advantage of most travelifts is that they can veer and haul the slings separately and on each side of the boat, allowing the hull to be tilted fore and aft and athwartships before being set down in the winter quarters berth – thus eliminating the need to get the trim right at the instant of starting to hoist in the water. Modern transport systems have made the job of moving boats so simple that a short paragraph suffices to describe them. But there is another, much more complicated, issue – often one that few boatowners have given any serious thought to.

Craning out, transporting, storing – who bears the responsibility?

Hauling unwieldy, wet and awkward boats and yachts out of the water, transporting them overland to their winter quarters, and setting them down safely is, when you consider it, a pretty difficult and even dangerous business. And although nowadays modern technology has substantially reduced the manpower requirements of the past and makes everything look so easy, yachts do still fall out of slings, boats topple from trailers, and crew or yard personnel break bones. It is then, if not before, that questions have to be answered about competence and expertise, about responsibility, about liability and damages.

Where these risks are taken by professionals, the situation is fairly clear: from the moment when the owner 'hands over' his craft to the yard crane operator, the risk and thus the responsibility for that valuable piece of goods is transferred to the yard and its staff. The yard is of course insured – imagine a crane driver replacing a £40,000 boat that he's ruined by dropping it on to the jetty.

However, many harbourmasters, club executive committees and indeed owners who might be affected are a lot less clear about the risk and its consequences. A court will consider every case on its own merits. Using the sequence of events involved in the transport of a boat, we will however endeavour to show here what might happen.

Let's assume that an owner puts his craft underneath the club crane in order to convey it to its winter quarters with the aid of the other club members. The moment he steps ashore and his colleagues, divided into teams, rig the slings, hoist the boat out of the water, set it on a trolley, push it into the shed and set it down there, the responsibility for the transport transfers to the club. However, as the owner is a club member and has agreed that his colleagues handle the boat, it is the owner's insurance company who will pay any damages, not the club. The Merchant Shipping Act states that a Master is always responsible for the care of his vessel and the owner is Master unless he specifically designates otherwise.

In a members' club, the committee is elected by the members; the owner is a member and therefore he is jointly responsible for the selection of the lifting team. However, if the team consists of a club's permanent employees and the crane is the property of the club, the club's indemnity insurance will cover the damage.

To avoid unpleasant, protracted and often unsuccessful disputes, all one can really do is urge all boatowners most strongly to take out a hull insurance that covers overland transport, including craning and laying up. It pays for own-boat damage. It does not cover personal injury, however, but this may well be covered by a separate policy.

Any possibility of an attempt to involve the club committee as being transport contractors for the yachts moved on their instructions should furthermore be excluded by a 'dispensation from liability' which the owners may have to give the club in writing. Its wording should be something like:

'I..., owner of the yacht..., hereby declare that in the event of material damage, personal injury or financial loss relating to my boat, myself or my family I will attribute no liability whatever to the ... club, its committee, its members or any other persons acting under the club's direction; not even if the damage, injury or loss was caused by gross negligence.'

Now the only possibility is that the authorities might step in because of a suspicion that a criminal act was involved. But that's another chapter, and one that doesn't belong in this book.

Other activities when craning out

Cleaning the underwater hull

Antifouling paint for the underwater hull can nowadays be relied on to ensure that, in most cases, our boats are fairly clean when they come out of the water.

The effectiveness of these paints, be they poisonous or not, hard or soft, insoluble or self-polishing, does however depend on a number of factors that individually or in combination are responsible for the appearance of growth in spite of the paint thickness being right and correct application. Among these factors are the degree of contamination, particularly with sewage, of the waters being sailed in; the hours of sunshine during the sailing season (light promotes growth); the position of the berthed boat relative to incoming light (stronger growth on illuminated side); and of course the length of time under way and the average speed. Many's the owner who has been astounded at the heavy growth on the submerged hull of his craft in spite of the large amount of money spent on paint to prevent precisely this. Coatings of algal slime, seaweed, barnacles or even mussels must obviously be removed. This should be done as soon as the crane has hoisted the craft out of the water, while it is still wet. Barnacles, in particular, are as hard as porcelain once dry; furthermore, they have such sharp edges that they can often only be chipped off with a chisel – a process that can result in the adjoining hull becoming scratched.

To do this cleaning, no appliance is more suitable than the high-pressure jet nozzle which here, as distinct from when using it on deck, can be confidently used at full pressure. Only in the case of planked wooden hulls is some caution necessary, to avoid blasting caulking out from the seams. Since any salt is also harmful to the underwater hull, the cleaning is best done with fresh water. The high pressure can be relied on to remove algae, seaweed and most of the barnacles and mussels; any stubborn barnacles need removing with a piece of wood (or with the handle of the scrubber). And remember also to turn the rudder, to reach the barnacles between the blade and the skeg/keel.

But that's not all the high water pressure does: it also extracts half-dissolved, oxidized and thus ineffective paint remains from the lattice structure of modern antifouling paint. And lastly, it indicates where the paint is not adhering properly, by exposing the hull skin underneath it; a fresh coat of paint will be required in any such places.

Having been jet cleaned, the underwater hull should be so clean that when it is dry it can be re-painted – and, in the case of self-polishing paint, without any preliminary sanding.

Disposing of poisonous material

Since environmental protection and other green issues have entered into the popular conscience, boatowners are seeing the world around them with new eyes: they have an increasing sense of guilt in the light of the poisonous brew that the high-pressure jet washes off from the underwater hulls of our vessels. This mix soaks into the soil or runs concentrated into the water in the harbour, and the (so far mostly poisonous) heavy metals such as tin and copper in the underwater paints may here and there get into the ground water. Boat-storage areas have, after many years of washing down and sanding, become heavily charged poisonous-waste deposits.

There have long been laws against such polluting of the environment. Most yards provide a skip or bins into which rubbish including paint waste is tipped, and from where it is taken to a chemical land fill site. Many places where boats are washed have collecting troughs or sumps that allow collection and purification of poisonous washing water; indeed, if possible, they are part of a closed circuit in which the same water is used several times. In many yards paint wash run-off seems not to be a problem, most of the water running from hard standing into drains or from gravel acting as a soak-away. However, legislation may well come into play on this matter. Clearly, the waste has to be disposed of properly. And we who engage in water sports must comply with these regulations if we are not to risk having to accept sweeping restrictions from higher authorities.

There is also a challenge to the paint industry: to develop environment-friendly and yet effective antifouling paints. Some initial success can be reported; tin-free underwater paint is already available. And we might possibly soon be relieved entirely of that tedious and expensive disposal procedure, if the attempts succeed to develop a gel coat that deters growth without needing painting. It is said to contain powdered copper which deters algae and barnacles without polluting in the process.

Cleaning the rest of the hull

While we are working on the underwater hull with the high-pressure cleaning appliance, it is useful to give the outside of the hull above the waterline a fresh-water shower. In this way, the underside of the (wooden) rubbing strake gets a particularly thorough and careful clean; this task is more difficult if done later on in winter quarters, using a brush (or indeed glass paper), and is liable to leave scratches on the hull.

Often the most stubborn grime is firmly stuck on in the region of the waterline (ie where oily harbour water leaves its grubby deposits). Even the high-pressure cleaning appliance can't remove such grime by itself. Help can be provided with a scrubber dipped in fine sea sand – but only on the underwater paint, not on the painted waterline or indeed the hull above. And anyway, the final cleaning and preservation of the above-water hull is left until the boat is in winter quarters.

Removing centreplate, rudder and prop shaft

In the case of centreplaters and keel-and-centreplate vessels, a check on the boards is often only possible while the boat is still hanging from the crane. Once such a craft is resting on its laying-up cradle, you can't usually lower the plate completely or indeed remove it. Something similar applies to keel craft where the rudder has to be removed downwards or the prop shaft backwards. Rather than waiting until the boat is in winter quarters and digging a deep hole in the ground under the stern, or sawing the cradle apart to dismantle the rudder or the shaft, you should use the opportunity provided by craning out to carry out that work now – having made appropriate preparations of course.

The sole of the keel, on which the vessel is later going to stand for a matter of months, is also visible and available to be worked on only once a year. So you should at least give it a quick visual check while the boat is still suspended above the ground.

From crane to winter quarters

Transport by mobile crane or travelift

One of the simplest, safest and time-saving ways of transporting a boat from where the crane has hoisted it out of the water to its winter quarters is to do so with the same crane. Simple, because the additional chore of transfer to a transporter or trolley is eliminated; safe, because during the journey, the boat is safe from tipping over in slings or damage from the lifting gear; time-saving, because there is no transferring, pushing about by hand, or connecting up of towing vehicles. What does have to be taken into account as a disadvantage is that while acting as transport, the mobile crane or travelift keeps other boats awaiting its return to where the hoisting is done. Further-more, laying-up berths in storage sheds are mostly not accessible to mobile cranes because of the height of the crane jib, and travelifts too lose their manoeuvrability where the free surface area is restricted, because they can't get close enough to (or away from) the neighbouring boat already set down.

For that reason, most winter-quarter operators combine procedures. Mobile cranes are used where boats can be set down directly within the swivelling range of the highly extendable crane jibs, the crane possibly needing to be shifted several times in the course of a day. They use travelifts for short trips between hoisting basin and shed; outside the shed, the boats are transferred to special trolleys which take them to their laying up berth where they are again, and finally, transferred to their storage cradle.

Transport by special vehicle

The days when moving boats – and particularly larger-keel yachts – overland was a nerve-wracking and extremely dangerous business have largely gone. In the past, a large number of helpers had at one and the same time to provide support for the boat and lay down rollers (tree trunks, steel pipes) for pushing it over sandy and uneven surfaces of open-air stowage areas and shed floors, all the time with the danger of the vessel tipping over. Not infrequently, this meant several weekends of extremely hard work for the owners.

Nowadays, things are easier: almost every water-sports club and professional body dealing with boats has special solutions to the transport problem. The simplest form of these is a trolley on which the boat's laying-up cradle is brought underneath the crane so that cradle and boat can then be moved to the laying-up berth. Once there, cradle and boat are raised a few centimetres using manually operated mechanical winches or hydraulic jacks; the trolley is then pulled out from under the cradle, and finally cradle and boat are set down on blocks. This procedure minimizes the capital outlay on the trolley; it also means that each vessel can be transported on its own, made-to-measure, cradle.

The minimum requirements for such simple trolleys are solid-tyre wheels individually steerable and lockable pointing 'fore and aft' and 'athwartships', removable sole bars and comprehensive galvanizing against corrosion. The minimum requirements for the cradles are that they must fit on to the trolley lengthwise and widthwise and be designed for the application of winches or hydraulic jacks.

A trolley that can be dismantled, comprising two axle units, two longitudinal girders and fitted with universally steerable solid rubber tyres, makes transporting boats much easier. The trolley is assembled or dismantled in position underneath the boat's transport cradle. All connections are made using socket-pins with handgrips, so no tools are needed.

Beyond this simple solution there are many more advanced ones, the most elegant – but also most expensive – being hydraulic low-lift platform trucks combined with all-purpose cradles. The trolley is often a three-wheeler with only the single front wheel steerable, and needn't be capable of dismantling because the sole bars with the two rear wheels are, as it were, run into the cradle. The cradle with or without the boat is raised by four hydraulic jacks operating together, supplied by a pump mounted on the trolley (power supply from own batteries or plugged-in cable). The outer supports on the all-purpose cradles are short lateral brackets located in line with the jacks. So that the cradles can take boats of differing size and construction (hull shape, draught, deadrise), these supports must be individually adjustable at least for height. If the intention is also to transport keel and centreboard boats and shallow-draught motorboats on such cradles, additional adjustable trestles are used as the main weight carriers.

Raised in this way the loaded cradles are moved – usually by tractor or by fork-lift which also moves the empty cradles around – accurately to the nearest centimetre into their laying-up berth where they are set down directly, without any blocks, on the ground/floor in the open air/shed.

This last method substantially reduces the manpower and time required to get a boat into its winter quarters. Comparing costs, however, makes it quite clear who can afford which of the two transport systems described. While a second-hand simple transport truck can be had for some £1000–£2000, a hydraulic low-lift platform truck (second-hand) will easily swallow £3000–£6800. That rules out the latter solution for many clubs, provided there is the manpower to replace the sophisticated technology. The situation is similar as regards all-purpose cradles, which in series production cost £250 to £500 each; thus for many owners they are too expensive to justify scrapping their own aged but sturdy wooden cradle.

Transport using your own trailer

Anyone owning a trailer for his boat is fortunate, for that eliminates all the questions, problems and expenses of transport overland and of the storage cradle. The boat is simply lowered on to the trailer by the crane and towed to its winter quarters. As against the advantages of this solution, the disadvantages are few. For instance, trailers or other transport vehicles you own that have inflated tyres should themselves be set up on blocks over the winter to save the tyres. And again, the suspension of such vehicles represents something of a hazard in that it can allow boat and trailer frame to start swaying in a gale and possibly tip over. And lastly, access to underwater hull

A shrewd, manpower-saving solution to the problem of transporting a boat is this three-wheeled trolley. The low-lift platform trolley carries an all-purpose cradle. Hydraulic jacks with return springs lift the cradle and boat, the jacks acting on lateral brackets on the cradle. The photograph shows the boat just about to be lifted.

Boat-transporter licensed for public roads. The keel sits in a deep trough and thus contributes to keeping the unit centre of gravity as low as possible. Anyone driving such a vehicle on the public roads must of course have an appropriate licence.

and keel is usually more awkward with a trailer, which makes overhaul somewhat more laborious.

Acquiring a suitable trailer for your own boat is simple enough, provided you can buy one ready made; for boats of all types up to a weight of about 1.5 tonnes, there is an abundance of trailers series produced by well-known manufacturers. These are affordable and, since they may be used on public roads, are also usable for transport to winter quarters farther away.

Where it is a matter of large bulk and short journeys, many owners get themselves 'retired' lorry chassis or trailers, converted and matched to the boat by welding on girders and brackets, though this can be expensive. Naturally, the greatest of care is needed here: the carrying capacity of both the vehicle and the added component parts and the quality of the welds has to be checked by experts (trained welders) to ensure there are no nasty surprises later on. For any sizeable boat you would need overrun brakes and a heavy towing vehicle.

You may consider the once-only expenditure on a trailer of your own worthwhile, since it makes you independent of appointments with cranes, helpers, and thus expenses. So long as the manager of your winter quarters accepts owners' trailers (in shed storages they are often not accepted because of their greater space requirement), they're worth considering.

A small trailer – up to 20 foot capacity – would cost around £800, less if second-hand, but they are not easy to find as the demand for them is great. The upper limit for practical towing without a Land Rover or similar vehicle is about 26 feet, if light displacement.

Ensuring your boat is standing safely ashore

The requirements of support systems

Curious as this may sound, a boat standing on land is subject to higher mechanical loading than when it is in water. For one thing, its entire weight is supported on a few small contact surfaces under the keel and along the hull. For another, out in the open there are added loads from roof structures and tarpaulins, snow, and people working on board. Lastly, stresses are introduced as a result of the hull bending the opposite way to that in the water.

The opinion held by many owners – that a keel and its suspension are the strongest components of a boat – has been brought into question by modern design concepts. Many boats lightly built to current designs already sag visibly when hanging from the crane, and must on no account go through the winter standing on their keels. Also, shells are often so thin that lateral shores dent them. Look out for advice about this in the handbook or, if in doubt, consult the yard or the designer.

On the other hand, for all other boats, the principle is valid that the keel carries the main load and lateral shores merely

A lightly built yacht like this modern 'racer' cannot be left to stand on its keel only – the hull must be supported by additional beams or girders.

the minimal side loads arising from inadequate horizontal squaring off of the vessel, from wind loading, or from people on board. Long-keel boats present the least problems because there is a large surface for transferring the hull-weight load. Fin-keelers with long hulls and extensive overhang should be provided with a stout shore fore and aft to prevent hogging.

The fewer the access-impeding shores, the easier the work on underwater hull, keel and rudder – something to be considered when setting down a boat ashore. You may have to dismantle the centreboard, rudder or prop shaft, which requires a minimum clearance between vessel and ground.

Setting-up on blocks and shoring up the hull

Boatowners usually have either their own cradles or one provided by the winter quarters operator, on which the craft can spend

A correctly stacked pile of 10 × 10 centimetre blocks of squared timber with a wooden cradle standing on it. Alternatively, one or two large blocks will serve.

the winter safely and with the loads properly distributed. Merely very large sailing- and motor-yachts whose LOA exceeds 16 metres are often conventionally set on blocks and shored up from the sides. Since this form of 'safe keeping' involves a lot more danger for the vessel than the rigid cradle, the job has to be done with great care. The sole of the keel has to be a sub-structure, more or less elaborate as may be necessary for it to carry and transfer to the ground the main load from the boat. That on the one hand must prevent with certainty the vessel sinking into the ground (something that can happen even with paved or tarmac floors); on the other, it should provide access to the sole to some extent for maintenance and painting. So the best thing to do is to build up two or more – depending on length and shape of the keel sole – piles of blocks of stout squared timbers (minimum cross-section for boats up to about 10 tonnes, 10 × 10 centimetres; more for larger) stacked alternately lengthwise and crosswise up to the desired height. The timbers are loaded in bending and shear by the weight of the boat, and so should be laid as close together as possible – the top ones obviously at right angles to the keel. If there is a danger of the boat sinking into the ground, the piles have to be stood on wooden boards, planks or steel plates to spread the weight.

If a dead-flat keel sole has more than two piles erected under it, then what is called a statically indefinite system is set up: it may then be that only two of the piles are bearing. This has to be checked by attempting to rock each pile; if necessary, two or four slim wedges must then be driven between the non-bearing pile and the keel.

Even more care is needed when laterally shoring a boat set up on blocks, because it must be established that each of the shores around the craft is bearing about the same load and – even more important – that none 'lets go' by just toppling over. Since

A whole lot of round-timber lateral shores is intended to keep this large boat standing securely. Wooden wedges are needed to ensure even loading of the individual shores.

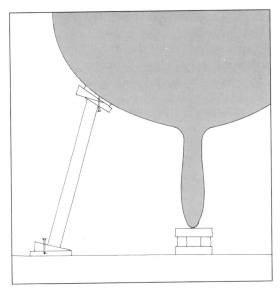

Securing the wedges used with the lateral shores: nails ensure the wedges can't work loose. The nails are not knocked in all the way so that in the spring they are easy to pull out with pincers.

shores generally are only relatively slim round poles 8–20 centimetres in diameter, the danger of their digging into the ground or making a dent in the hull is considerable. Even worse, they are inclined, and thus transfer the load on them to the ground only via an edge; thus they need to have, as appropriate, a large-area 'underlay' between them and the ground and/or be cut off at an angle or wedged. Wedges should also be used at the hull end, or the plain shore may scratch the surface as it is being positioned. It is important to secure all wedges by nailing them down, but leave the nail head projecting about a centimetre so that the nails can be pulled out again with pincers. Caution and a light touch are the watchword when positioning shores, as follows: once the boat is standing level with the keel on the piles of blocks, a first pair of shores is placed amidships, on the port and starboard sides. These two shores are intended to bear the principal load due to any tilting movement of the hull and may therefore be stressed as highly as possible by means of wedges. Next, two more shores are rigged towards the fore and aft end of the hull respectively, whose wedges must be driven in with the greatest of care because here again a statically indefinite system is set up: the more load one shore takes, the more the adjoining one becomes unloaded until it finally falls down! So, going progressively around the boat, you drive in the wedges carefully until all the shores are carrying as near as possible the same load, which has to be checked by rocking them carefully. Then secure the wedges – and *never, never* fasten any of the lines from the tarpaulin to a shore!

These lateral shores in particular must be checked frequently for correct position and load while the boat is laid up, and the wedges possibly 'hardened up' and re-secured. There is a lot less worry with a rigid cradle.

However, anyone who (whether for reasons of cost or of storage difficulties over the summer) can't make up his mind whether to have a rigid cradle might for the time being consider

If there is no ready-made cradle available, a makeshift version can be produced by joining up the lateral shores using wooden battens. Wooden wedges ensure an even distribution of the load. The connections are nailed.

an intermediate solution: this is arrived at by linking and nailing together the four or six lateral shores that have been cut to size and matched to the hull, using long battens. If the keel is supported on thick planks instead of piled blocks, these planks can be embodied in the structure. A temporary cradle cobbled together in this way is easily taken apart again in the spring by pulling out the nails, and is not difficult to stow. The individual timbers should be marked before dismantling to facilitate re-use.

Storage cradles

A rigid cradle is simple to operate, and safe for the boat and the crew working on it, but has the disadvantages that it is costly to buy and takes up space in the summer. In the past,

All-purpose cradles have to be made in such a way that their lateral shores are extensively adjustable. This cradle will take boats ranging in length from 7 to 12 metres.

All-purpose cradles can even take shallow-draught boats
without any keel. An additional trestle of appropriate height is
inserted to take the weight of the boat.

rigid cradles were mostly constructed in wood, but nowadays
they are made from I-beams, steel box-profiles, and steel tubes,
assembled and welded together. Protection against corrosion is
obtained by using galvanized material (attention – before welding, remove zinc from the vicinity of the welds!) or by subsequent
painting with anti-rust paint (red lead, epoxy-tar) and enamel.
There are two main types: first, the (adjustable) all-purpose
cradle with standard base dimensions, required to fit on to the
special transport-/low-lift platform truck, but at the same time
to adjust as necessary to the shape of the underwater hull and
the draught. And secondly, the special cradle, fitting only your
own craft. Which of these two you choose is often not just a
matter for you to decide. Professional operators of winter quarters who aim to rationalize the work of accepting and delivering
yachts as far as possible to minimize costs, often insist on use
of the all-purpose cradle which the owner has to rent or buy
outright. In most clubs, however, the special cradle still
dominates.

Whichever is the case, prior to purchasing a storage cradle or having one built, planning and measurement will at any rate be necessary to establish carrying capacity and dimensions. The first element to come up for consideration is the keel bearer. The starting point for this is that a 'normal' boat transfer 100 per cent of its overall weight via the keel to the cradle and thence to the ground (ie rests exclusively on the keel). This is the case at least until the lateral shores take an – admittedly minimal – share, at most 5 per cent, of the load, if indeed they are so rigged under the hull that they take any at all. If in the winter quarters the cradle with the boat is to stand raised on four piles of blocks, then both the keel bearer and the associated horizontal girders have to be designed to take the entire weight. Additionally, people working on board, hand and machine tools, and in the open a roof structure, tarpaulin, and loading from

This is an acceptable form of boat cradle. It couldn't be simpler: from the ends of the channel girders four chains run up to deck level, with steel clips to hook on to the toerail. Tensioned by means of rigging screws, they keep the boat upright.

snow and wind have to be allowed for; furthermore, dynamic loads can arise due to the boat swaying. For these reasons, load-bearing parts should be designed to take 150 per cent of the calculated load. The establishment of dimensions is easier if the cradle is intended to rest exclusively with its entire base on level, portative (ie reinforced) floors: the weight of the boat does not then apply a bending stress to the keel, which allows its dimensions to be reduced substantially. This, however, means that while boat and cradle are being transported, the lateral shores are loaded more heavily, under a buckling load.

Taking any risks in the calculations for the design of a cradle is totally unacceptable. Though many a boatowner when selecting girders, profiles and tubes works 'by guess and by God' and by crossing his fingers, it is better to leave the calculations to a designer of steel structures. On the basis of his guidelines and regulations, he may well 'overdimension', but the result is your peace of mind. Similarly, any welding should be done by a trained

A variously adjustable storage cradle which can be collapsed to save space when not needed. The chains absorb tensile loads which may come on to the lateral shores, particularly during transport overland.

welder. Scrap merchants can be helpful in obtaining materials, charging usually only a fraction of what one would have to pay for new parts. But look out – a little rust on scrap is acceptable, but heavily rusted material is not. Here also you should use the services of an expert, who will check the scrap for dimensional accuracy with his sliding calipers; if there is significant rusting, he will at once subtract 10 per cent of the carrying capacity.

Here are a couple of tips when designing a storage cradle, which help to make life in winter quarters easier. First, try to retain easy access to the underwater hull by dispensing with framing longitudinals. The base can just as well look like a double 'T', the lateral shores standing on its four corners. Should these shores interfere with storage during the summer, make them collapsible with adjustable chains for when they are in use. Also, the adjustment and loading of the lateral shores underneath the underwater hull becomes very easy if the shores

Owners who are considering building a storage cradle for their boat in the near future can learn something here. The structure, made from box-section steel girders, is not only lightweight, it also makes for comfortable working on the underwater hull by virtue of not having any framing longitudinals.

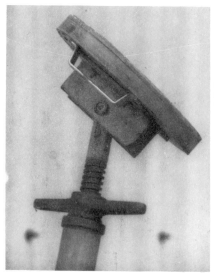 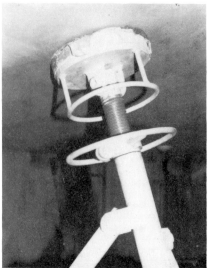

Adjustable shores as part of boat storage cradles. On the left, with tilting pins; on the right, with fine-lead square thread. For safety there are handles to stop hands getting between the hull and the disc on the shore when the boat is being set down.

are fitted with threaded elements at the upper end. That sort of thing can be obtained from the building trade, where it is sold for use in foundation work (trenching).

Accidents in winter quarters

This book would be incomplete without some reference to the dangers that face the transporting team – be they yard experts or club amateurs – when moving multi-tonne-weight boats about, and the hazards encountered by those who work on the craft during the winter.

The most common injuries when transporting boats overland occur during craning out: anyone forced to remain within the swivelling orbit of a crane (something actually forbidden by the regulations for the prevention of accidents) is all too liable to be struck by a swinging crane cable with its heavy block or hook, by a wire strop, or 'merely' by a sling – result: injury to head, shoulders or back. A hard hat may prevent the worst damage, but concentration and alertness at all times are essential. Next most frequent injuries are those to the hands because of 'meat hooks' in wire ropes and contusions where hands have got between boat and sling. For this reason, personal equipment should include a stout pair of rigger's gloves.

As soon as trucks carrying boats move off, there is the danger of their tyres running over the feet of bystanders or those pushing the vehicle – steerable wheels in particular have already squashed many a sailor's foot beyond recovery. So wear safety boots with steel toecaps – and always keep an eye on the nearest wheel or, rather, the man at the drawbar who is steering the truck.

And when the boat is at last safely in its laying-up berth, that's usually the start of an interminable succession of climbs. Via a ladder (and over the guardrails), you will have to keep climbing on board to remove equipment. Make it your unbreakable rule to secure the top of the ladder to the craft (toerail, pushpit, etc) before the very first climb, to stop it falling over or toppling backwards together with a heavily laden person. It's equally dangerous to untie, or even just to slack back, the guardrail wires: anyone who has been in the habit all summer of grabbing the rail for support will grab the wire in winter quarters too. Wherever possible, you should lean the ladder against the stern, lash it to the pushpit, and climb on deck through the opening in the latter.

And do remember too, when working on deck, that a boat in its storage cradle is capable of short, sharp tilting movements that one isn't accustomed to, movements that can easily tip one over the side on to the ground. Any resulting broken bones and head injuries are often extra dangerous because there are few helpers around, or none at all.

The second skin: preserving the boat

Cleaning the hull

I expect you've noticed that a large part of this book is concerned with cleaning your boat. The reason for this is that dirt holds moisture – and moisture has no place on board in winter quarters. That is why, now that the vessel is safely in its laying-up berth, we turn to the thorough clean of the shell of your craft. Cleaning, though, is not the same as preserving; the two processes should be separated. Advertisements make great claims for all sorts of two-in-one cleaners that contain wax as well as dirt removers (mostly solvents), and these certainly do make the work easier. However, they have the disadvantage that many a damaged place in the gel coat (eg hair- and star-cracks, minor scratches and holes) goes undetected because it is filled with wax and simply plastered over. Repairing and painting shells so treated (and that applies also to enamelled steel/varnished wooden hulls) is impossible because the preservative wax rejects any gel coat, filler or paint. So, to start with, clean the shell thoroughly.

Where the fouling is slight, you can use (soft) soap and water; for fender marks and oily or greasy residues, try one of the special GRP- and enamel/varnish cleaners without preservative (a wide range of which are offered by the yacht-accessory trade). Very stubborn dirt around the waterline or the engine exhaust may require strong grease-solvent cleaners (often with a tetrachloroethylene base – use with care on the painted-on waterline!).

Brown discoloration of the gel coat on GRP boats can usually be bleached or removed with more or less strongly diluted hydrochloric acid (1:20 to 1:5; be careful – wear gloves and rinse well afterwards). The last resort if all else fails is polishing the gel coat away with polishing paste on a sponge-plastic polishing disc, applied using a hand drill set to slow-running, with moderate pressure, until you have a spotless gel coat. Following this thorough cleaning, you have to rinse well with lots of clean water to remove any remains of soap or cleaning debris. When all this has been done, you can examine the 'naked' shell to check for damage to the gel coat or the varnish.

Damage that has to be repaired at once

If the clean hull shows minor damage that could spread further, repairable at little cost in terms of time and materials, then you should get on with repairs straight away. Hair- and star-cracks in the gel coat, shallow scratches and holes all need scraping out at once – possibly down to the gel – and then filling with gel coat repair material prior to smoothing down.

Damage to paint on steel vessels – enamel flaking off, scratches and cracks – must be checked for rust which, unless checked, will spread under the loose paint during the laying-up period. So remove all loose paint; should this reveal rust, treat it at once with chemical rust converter as a precautionary measure (this will protect it until the spring).

Wooden-hulled boats need equally careful inspection for damage to the varnish. Light-coloured, blistery areas on surfaces with clear varnish are a sign that moisture has been able to penetrate the varnish layer and has lifted it away from the wood. A blackened area may already have started to develop there, and this will spread during the winter. Coloured varnish makes it harder to spot such blisters, but their removal is just as important. Blackened wood under the defective varnish should be bleached or removed immediately with glass paper or a scraper and the raw wood revealed should be preserved with antirot compound – which the producers of boat paints keep especially for this purpose. If, however, larger-scale rot shows up in wooden-hulled vessels, action must under no circumstances be delayed until the spring because bacterial/fungal decay spreads rapidly. Rotten wood must be removed completely by cutting, grinding or scraping out. The adjoining sound wood must then be saturated with antirot compound.

In recent years, a problem that has been arising increasingly is the so-called osmotic blistering on synthetic-hulled boats. Although it only shows up as small blisters in the gel coat and is almost always restricted to the underwater hull, it is certainly not 'minor damage'. If note is not taken of it in the autumn when preparing for the winter, the damage will spread considerably – particularly if there are severe frosts. As a result of osmosis, water has been able to penetrate through the gel coat into the GRP underneath.

This water must be got out as quickly as possible to stop it spreading further, and to prevent damage to the hull if it freezes. So the dried-off underwater hull is inspected minutely for blisters, which can be pricked to allow evaporation of the water that has penetrated. Later, the blistered gel coat must be removed to expose the glass fibre so that it can dry out thoroughly. The only justification for not doing this is when the GRP hull is already so extensively affected by osmotic blistering that the whole of the underwater hull is going to have to be renewed anyway – which is only rarely possible during laying up because the special procedures involved call for a heated (or summer-warm) shed.

Once all minor damage to the boat has been made good (or at least treated), one last, sweaty, job remains: preserving the craft against all the rigours of the winter.

Preservation

The second skin that is applied to all synthetic-material surfaces of a boat as a protective layer (and that can also protect coats of paint on wooden- and steel-hulled vessels, provided they are in good condition and don't require renewal) has two purposes. The first is to protect the surface coating, whether gel coat, paint or varnish, against the penetration of moisture. The second function is to ward off sanding dust, paint splashes from the next-door boat, and dirt from the air.

Moisture accumulates on all external surfaces, primarily from sweating: if the sun shines on to a boat storage shed or a 'tent' out in the open, the ice-cold hulls 'drip with sweat'. This water penetrates through the gel coat and paint, which are by no means impervious to water unless protected. For boats in the open without cover, rain and fog have the same effect. Add frost to this, and you have pre-programmed damage in the form of minute fissures in the gel coat or paint.

Protective coatings can be applied either as wax or as resin, depending on the effort you are prepared to make and available finances. The simplest and cheapest way is to use one of the variety of boat waxes obtainable. This is applied with a sponge to the dry, clean surface. The sponge should be a real one, because the solvents in some of the cleaning waxes attack and soften synthetic sponges. Once the liquid wax has dried, you will see a dull, usually greyish-white or brown, coating that you then wipe over with soft cloths or cotton wool, making circular movements and applying a bit of pressure. The dry wax particles have a polishing effect, albeit only a slight one, and this gives a splendid shine – provided the plastic or varnished/painted surface is in good condition (ie not 'chalky' or inherently dull).

The more laborious-to-apply and also more expensive protective coating is obtained by using preservatives containing resins in solution, or indeed consisting entirely of liquid synthetic resins. Whereas simple boat waxes provide effective protection for barely a few months, using liquid acrylic resin means boats can be properly 'sealed' for a matter of years. However, the success of such resins presupposes absolute compliance with the relevant application instructions, plus the right temperature and humidity conditions; a casual approach will produce a streaky and patchy finish.

Incidentally, apart from providing protection for plastic and painted surfaces, waxes and resins are also useful for metal parts: they can equally well be used to protect pushpits and pulpits and guardrail stanchions. But don't let either of them get on to untreated wood (teak decks, handrails, gratings) because the white coating they would leave behind in the pores of the wood is often very hard to remove. Finally, here is a tip that never fails to be greeted with astonishment: using a piece of cut-pile carpet (20 × 20 centimetres square) for polishing wax not only makes child's play of the job, but also results in a better shine.

Protection from the weather

There are many boatowners, particularly in northern Europe, who consider all the wrapping up, covering over, and providing the vessel with a roof in winter quarters to be totally unnecessary. Such owners let their boats stand ashore just as they lie in the water, where they are exposed to rain and sunshine, grime and salt. Is this foolish? What, after all, can happen to a well-maintained plastic-hulled boat whose deck and hull have had a protective coating of wax applied? Well – as has already been pointed out elsewhere – it's not so much the (rain-water) that savages boats, but the ice. Everywhere on board there are gaps, cracks and openings (eg around bolted-on windows, bilge drainpipes, underneath covers and flaps, in teak decks) where ice can do damage as it increases in volume with falling temperatures. An ice-filled cockpit whose engine instrumentation and steering gear pedestal, companionway and locker seats stay frozen up for weeks, the substantial weight of ice additionally loading the hull and the cradle, is surely not something either the designer or the boatbuilder had in mind.

So, if you love your boat, cover it carefully with a tarpaulin. However, there are various viewpoints as to how best to do this – each way has advantages and disadvantages.

The 'tight-wrapping' method

Have you ever visited the storage area of a large boatbuilding yard, where brand-new vessels sit awaiting transport to the dealer or buyer? If so, you will have noted, maybe with surprise, that the boats are often totally wrapped in welded-up transparent plastic sheet – just like chops in a deep freeze. If one could treat boats in the same way for laying up, this would be the ideal way to bring them perfectly preserved through the winter.

However, the tight-wrapping method offers almost equal protection against the weather, provided the work is planned and carried out with care. (Note that it is not ideal for wood as it can encourage any small areas of rot because it is impossible to achieve a totally dry seal.) The method is based on wrapping a tight-fitting tarpaulin around the boat without having to erect

This boat has been wrapped for laying up. The guardrails have been removed completely. The tarpaulin fits tightly around the boat and needs no roof-ridge. Built-in pockets take the pulpit and pushpit.

a roof structure for this beforehand. The tarpaulin should lie on the cabin roof, run to the deckedge (toerail, gunwale, rubbing strake) and enclose the hull down to the waterline.

At the same time, the above-deck part should slope like a roof so that snow can slide off. But you must be sure the tarpaulin does not chafe the deck or the hull at any point – that would leave dull and lustreless abraded patches, particularly on gel coat or varnished surfaces. Finally, fresh air must be able to flow through the boat in spite of the tight-fitting tarpaulin, to counteract condensation and rot. In listing these requirements for the tight-wrapping method, we have already hinted at the problems associated with it.

The first problem is that structures projecting a long way above the deck (eg the mast tabernacle, ventilator cowls, pushpit and pulpit) need either to be taken down or, better still, they should each project into a special pocket tailored to fit by the maker of the tarpaulin.

The second problem is as follows: to achieve the necessary slope of the tarpaulin over the deck and prevent rain or snow forming puddles on it, the whole of the guardrails (stanchions and intermediate wire as well) should be dismantled and the stanchion-foot fittings need to be well padded to stop them making holes in the tarpaulin.

The third drawback is this: to stop the tarpaulin chafing in windy weather, it has to be hauled taut by means of lines going through under the hull/keel, and to this end it must have a large number of sturdy eyelets (pressed-in brass or stainless-steel eye) around its lower edges. It is important to remember to pad these eyelets if necessary (using bits of foam, rags) so that they can't chafe the hull either.

And fourthly, in spite of the tight wrapping around the entire boat, openings as large as possible should be left at bow and stern to allow fresh air to get in under the tarpaulin and (via hatches left open a little?) flow into the vessel to prevent condensation and rotting. On the other hand, there must be no way that snow could get in through these ventilation openings. To ensure this, owners lash short lengths of piping (eg 200 millimetre diameter PVC pipe from the building- or sanitary-

This photograph illustrates a precaution that is well worth taking. Pieces of rag or, as here, small rolls of carpet material, jammed between the lashings and the hull prevent chafing which causes scratches or dull areas in the gel coat.

equipment trade) into the tarpaulin, projecting beyond it at bow and stern and inclined downwards. The dimensions of the 'wrapping-up tarpaulin' are most easily calculated by means of a sketch showing a cross-section of the hull in three places – forebody, midship section, cockpit. The length of the drawn lines from the waterline on one side over the deck/the superstructure to the waterline on the other side gives you the width of the tarpaulin. To be even safer, do the measuring directly on the boat in its cradle, with a long tape and two helpers. In fact, the person making the tarpaulin will visit the craft to do some expert measuring and, at the same time, to discuss whether, and if so where, it might be necessary to include pockets, folds or scoops.

Wooden rafter timbers are a popular, cheap and easy-to-work material for making a roof frame to spread the tarpaulin over. The uprights are lashed to the guardrail stanchions. The projecting ends of the rafters have to be padded carefully.

The finished tarpaulin, made from tough plastic sheet, will thus not be rectangular but rather oval, matching the shape of the boat. For a 10 metre yacht it will cost between £250 and £400, depending on material and finish. Properly made and used with care, it will last for many years.

The tight-wrapping method has many devotees in spite of its disadvantages. For instance, since removing and replacing such a tarpaulin is quite laborious, you won't often be climbing on board or working on the boat during the winter. Therefore the method suits GRP boats whose owners live far from the winter quarters, or don't need to do anything to the boat apart from giving it a fresh coat of antifouling.

Tarpaulin with a roof frame on deck

Much more expensive than the wrapping-up method described above is protecting a boat left in the open for the winter using a tarpaulin made into a tent by laying it on top of a proper roof frame.

The advantages of this method are obvious: access to outside and inside at all times and thus the possibility of making use of mild winter days for inspections or indeed overhaul, plus better ventilation. On the other hand, this roof-frame-plus-tarpaulin arrangement has its dangers: since it is erected on the deck, the wind-attack surface area and thus the load on the total system tarpaulin/boat/cradle is increased substantially. Should a strong wind get underneath the tarpaulin – which for improved ventilation and protection against chafing is usually rigged with an air gap right around the boat – then this whole structure may blow away or, even worse, tear the boat out of its cradle or topple it over.

There are many options for the design and construction of the roof frame, and you will see a number of different versions at the various winter quarters – not all of which can be dealt with here. From the many solutions you may see, we have selected just two.

One solution for a roof frame is very simple and low-cost, and the other is somewhat more expensive. Both, however, must meet certain minimal requirements: the roof must slope enough for snow to slide off and thus its enclosed angle must not exceed approximately 90 degrees; the structure must be sufficiently robust to withstand wind pressure and snow loading and be firmly anchored to the boat (ie not just set down on the deck); and there must be no possibility of either the tarpaulin or its securing lines chafing the vessel.

The simpler structure uses a single ridge pole (possibly the mast, substantially stripped bare), laid fore and aft from bow to stern. To get the required slope on the tarpaulin, this pole has to be at quite some height above the deck and, since pulpit and pushpit are usually not high enough to act as direct supports, the pole should rest on from three to six props set along the centreline. If the intention is not to dismantle the guardrails for the winter and to run the tarpaulin over them, the ridge pole has to be set up even higher. Lateral support is provided by means of ropes which, fastened to the pole with a clove hitch,

Above: these guardrails were taken down; their feet house the short roof supports instead of the stanchions. Below: the roof timbers are joined by means of flat, galvanized joining-brackets obtainable from builders' merchants.

are run athwartships to the toerail or the guardrail stanchion feet and set up hard. They later also act as the 'rafters' on which the tarpaulin rests.

Suitable material for pole and props is pressure-impregnated squared timber no less than 8 × 8 centimetres. To protect the tarpaulin, the pole should have its upper edges rounded off slightly using 20-grade glass paper. Since this sort of timber is not obtainable in the required length of, for example, 10 metres, and if it were, would not be transportable by car, the pole has to have a number of joins; the simplest way of making these is by means of lengths of galvanized thin-walled square tubing (square box section) from the ironmonger. The ridge pole is fastened to its props with appropriate lengths of nickel-plated wood screws going through the pole into the props. The props should stand on small squares of carpet. The cost of the entire simple structure is about £35. The individual parts are of course reusable.

What applied to the wrapping-tarpaulin applies to this one also: it should be oval, matching the shape of the boat, and have eyelets around the edges. An effective way of fastening the tarpaulin (once it is in position) to the boat is with lanyards to the (pierced) toerail or, failing that, to the feet of the guardrail stanchions. If, on the other hand, you use lines taken through under the hull, then once again precautions against chafing are necessary. If the tarpaulin is led over the top of the guardrails, then the rails/wire (and especially the top ends of the stanchion) should first be padded thoroughly; an appropriate length of cellular plastic tubing (pipeline insulating tubing from the plumbing trade), slit lengthways and fitted over the railings, is useful for this purpose. At bow and stern the edges of the tarpaulin come together to form a vertical 'seam', pulled together tightly with long lanyards through the eyelets and tied to the bow/stern fitting.

A more expensive roof structure, but one that is quick and easy to erect, consists of ready-made rafters either stuck into the feet for the guardrail stanchions if these have been removed, or lashed to the stanchions if they have not. These rafters are in fact proper tubular frames made from aluminium

These roof frames made from steel tubing are a bit more expensive to buy but are quick and easy to erect. They fit into the guardrail stanchion feet. An extra wire running through the bottom ends of the tubes all the way around the boat can be used to ensure a good fit of the tarpaulin which, to allow good ventilation of the boat, is kept clear of the hull.

or steel tubes bent/welded into shape. The ridge pole can be built up using the same tubes, connected up by means of cross sleeves, but it is sufficient to keep the frames the right distance apart with a continuous line secured to the boat at bow and stern.

A further major advantage of this type of covering is the method of fastening the tarpaulin edges: a stainless-steel wire (7 × 19/4 millimetre diameter) is drawn along inside the hem of the tarpaulin and fed through appropriately located drillings in the tube ends. This means there is no risk of anything chafing and the tarpaulin is lashed swiftly and safely.

Manufacture of the tubular frames is best left to a pipefitter who will be able to bend the tubes without kinks or creases and produce welds of a professional quality. Since these frames can't be made on a series-production basis – every frame has to be individually shaped according to the shape of the boat – the cost for a 10 metre craft (assuming six pairs of guardrail stanchions) is likely to be much the same as that for the tarpaulin; altogether, you thus have to expect the cost of covering the boat to be around £750. But for that price you do get a durable and really weatherproof system whose life will scarcely be less than that of the vessel itself. Work on deck and hull is possible at any time; there is no need to check the lashings and lines at regular intervals; and rigging and de-rigging the covering requires little effort.

The only superior method of protecting a boat laid up in the open is popping its own boathouse down over the top of it, and it is this that we look at in the next section.

Erecting a mini-boatshed

If you feel particularly benevolent towards your boat, are good with your hands, and are willing and able to spend more money, you will choose what is probably the most expensive solution to the problem of wintering your vessel in the open: you will put up a proper housing around the boat. However, do check local planning regulations if you decide to build one at home. This has a lot of advantages. Since the housing stands on the ground, it does not place any load on the boat or cradle. And there is no chance of the component parts, tarpaulin or lines damaging the vessel by chafing. Provided the housing is sufficiently roomy to allow access all around the boat and the tarpaulin reaches down to the ground, work on the shell and the underwater hull is possible at any time.

However, the design and construction of such a mini-boatshed do make pretty heavy demands on owner-builders and their helpers. First, the material has to be chosen. A cheap version would be a wooden structure for which so-called rafter timber (18 × 36 millimetre x-section, length up to 2.4 metres; obtainable from builder's merchants) can be used, provided the tarpaulin is not too large and heavy and the wind- and snow-loading to be expected not too great. Use of such rafter timbers is thus limited to smaller buildings intended for boats up to about 6 metres in length. To connect the individual timbers you can use nails, but you have to have a hefty lump of iron (or else a second hammer of at least 5 kilograms) handy as a dolly, because most of the nailing during assembly has to be done 'up in the air'. A serious disadvantage of the nailing method is that you can usually use the timbers only once or twice. A better method is as follows: each timber has a 6 millimetre hole drilled at the connection points, and bolts (M 6 × 100, brass or nickel-plated; washers under head and nut) are used for the assembly.

If you want the wooden parts of the structure to last, they have to be impregnated with a wood preservative.

Larger boats need a stronger wooden structure. The load-bearing parts (uprights, ridge beam) have to be 10 × 10 centimetre squared timber; all other parts need to be rafter timber or, where there will be only tensile loads, maybe thinner planks (eg 20 × 47 millimetre battens). A possible construction material other than wood is of course metal tubing, and the best solution here is aluminium tube with a diameter of about 60 millimetres, connected up by means of clips, claws and linkages. Such tubing

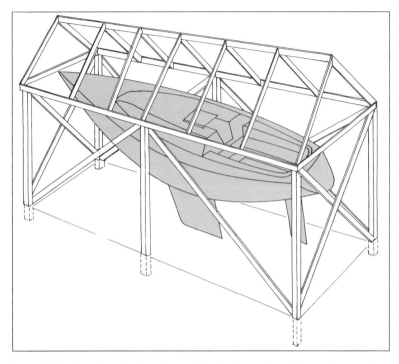

A sketch showing the basic method of construction of a small boat-storage shed. The parts are all either squared timber or rectangular or roof battens, and are held together by a wood-joining device of some kind. Bolts and nuts are recommended.

is obtainable – possibly reasonably priced second-hand – from scaffolding construction firms, large firms of decorators, or industrial concerns. Additionally, there are nowadays quite a few firms specializing in the manufacture and distribution of wooden and metal structures for protecting boats.

The second question to be answered before starting to design a mini-boatshed concerns how it is to be fastened to the ground – after all, it has to withstand gale-force winds. In principle, there are two possibilities: the uprights can either be buried in the ground or held down on it by heavy weights. Burying is of course laborious (holes for 10×10 squared timber: $30 \times 30 \times 70$ hole; after lowering in the uprights, refill with the dug-out earth and compact well by stamping) and, furthermore, it is not allowed on some laying up sites. If you use weights, the job is a bit easier. You can quite easily make them yourself by filling 5 or 10 litre plastic buckets with concrete (get ready-mixed from a building site) into which you stick a previously prepared steel stirrup (reinforcing steel from a firm catering for the reinforced-concrete construction industry) before it sets. In this way, you obtain portable weights of about 12 kilograms (5 litre bucket) or 25 kilograms (10 litre bucket). To be most effective, the weights are fastened directly to the tarpaulin after this has been rigged over the framework.

This brings us to the third important question: when and how do you put up the mini-boatshed? Erection of the shed comes after the boat has been set down on its laying up site, so that the vessel can be used as a construction platform for the shed's erection and assembly and for the final covering with the tarpaulin. Once that has been rigged properly, the weights are distributed around the boat and the tarpaulin secured to the stirrups on them by short lengths of rope. Indeed, some owners go one step further, in that they hang the weights from the tarpaulin so that they dangle freely above the ground, eliminating the need for periodic checks of the rope tension during the winter. If that is intended, to distribute the pull more evenly the tarpaulin should have extra-strong hems into which long square wooden battens could be inserted if desired.

Dimensions and structuring of the tarpaulin are derived from the dimensions of the building framework: it should extend to about a metre above the ground all round. The two ends will have long 'seams' fitted with eyelets, and each pulled shut by means of a long line which also has a weight fastened to its end.

When all this has been done, you will have a finished mini-shed. Because of its airy construction there will be no need for any special ventilation arrangements for either the shed or the vessel within it. If you hope to be doing a lot of work on your boat during the winter, you should provide good working conditions by choosing a tarpaulin material that is light-coloured and

The mini-boathouse with a galvanized-steel-tube frame is almost as good as a shed. The tarpaulin is secured perfectly and the 45 degree slope of the roof ensures that snow slides off. The tarpaulin would be better if it extended downwards another 1.5 metres.

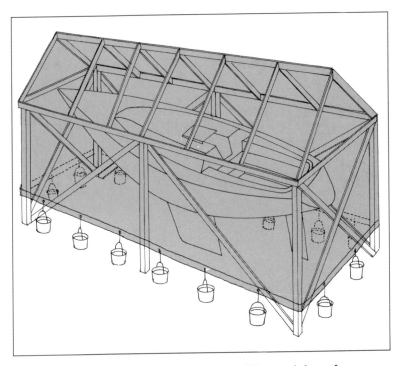

Weights can be used to help out, where the uprights of a
home-built boat shed cannot be let into the ground. Here,
concrete-in-plastic-bucket weights lashed to the hem of the
tarpaulin hold the structure firmly to the ground.

transparent. The owners most likely to adopt this laying-up
solution (bearing in mind the effort and expense) will probably
be those with the more labour-intensive wooden- and steel-hulled
craft. A complete timber framework for a 10 metre boat, made
by a professional, is likely to cost around £150, or around £500
if aluminium, a heavy tarpaulin another £200, or up to £500
plus if tailored, and the (8 to 10) weights around £50 so that
you end up with an average figure of £750. But that's still a
good deal cheaper than laying up in a large boat-storage shed
or farm barn: the difference in cost between laying up in a

boat-storage shed and in the open may be as much as £300 for the first winter alone, so that the cost of your own shed can be saved after three winters of not having to pay the large-shed rate. However, many boatyards will charge more for a boat stored under one of the above structures since the vessel will take up far more space.

Damage and danger to the boat in winter quarters

Once laid up, some owners may not see their boats again for many months. Their proud vessel, now looking rather like a sad mummy, is erased from their memory until they are struck by the first warming rays of the spring sun. It is then that such owners begin to wonder how much damage humidity and frost have caused to their boats. Sometimes, serious damage is caused by simple forgetfulness.

For example, one fine winter's day I did a routine check on board my boat stored in a shed, only to discover that a bottle of mineral water left behind in the saloon had exploded. Its splinters had made holes and tears in lampshades and curtains, had got into every single 'swallow's nest' and cupboard (the latter's doors naturally open for better airing), and fragments still kept turning up in the most unexpected places several seasons later.

Humidity is even worse. Any absorbent material not removed in the autumn – that is, bolsters, cushions, rugs, blankets, books, charts, curtains, carpets, clothing, shoes, etc – eagerly absorbs moisture from the air and begins to smell musty or, worse still, grows fungus or mould. Humidity also causes corrosion of engine parts, brass lamps/lanterns, electrical contacts and untreated wood. The only way to combat it is by adequate ventilation or, where that can't be guaranteed, by dehumidifying the air inside the boat.

Through-ventilation is easier for owners whose boats are lying in the open. As has been said already, openings have to be provided in the covering tarpaulin, and ventilators/hatches left open to ensure that wind generates a natural flow of air through the craft. Below deck all cupboards, lockers and drawers must be open, any seat cushions left behind set on edge, and underseat stowages also opened.

Note that all extensive tented structures, except those with a semi-circular section (rather like a Nissen hut) are very prone to wind damage. If wind can get under the cover at all it can be very troublesome, even dangerous.

In a laying up shed air won't naturally circulate through the boat. Artificial ventilation by an electric appliance (eg a fan heater set to 'cold') is not possible – both because of the cost of electricity and because many shed operators switch off the electricity for safety when there is no one in the shed. The latest type of boat ventilator, powered by solar cells, is unlikely to get enough light in the shed to function effectively. Because one of the major advantages of laying up in a shed is precisely that you don't have to clear everything out of the boat, effective dehumidification is essential. The type of dehumidifier whose salt filling dries out the air below deck, available for some years now, has proved effective for this. The water extracted from the air in this way collects in the bottom of the appliance and is emptied out at intervals of some weeks. In order for this to work effectively, hatches and ventilators have to be shut, otherwise the moisture in the surrounding air in the shed will immediately re-humidify the dry air inside the boat.

Precautions against frost damage have already been discussed elsewhere, so here we will simply repeat the advice: drain or remove from on board any water in tanks, pipelines, bilges and toilet, and of course all water-containing stores (drinks, tinned food, liquid cosmetics in glass bottles, etc). Where the water can't be got rid of entirely (bilge, toilet), some antifreeze will prevent damage.

The technical equipment on board shouldn't be neglected totally. For instance, the engine should be turned over a few times by hand at regular intervals to re-establish the protective film of lubricant in the bearings and on the cylinder walls.

The same applies to the reversing gearing and the prop shaft with its stern tube bearing, and even the sea cocks should be operated occasionally. Any (lead-acid) batteries left on board must always be fully charged, to protect them against extremely low temperatures and also to prevent sulphating of the plates making them faulty. But be careful, the detonating gas released during charging due to gassing of the batteries increases the fire risk. During charging and for several hours after, there must be no working on board with spark-generating tools or, perish the thought, naked flames. (Some insurance companies prohibit the use of battery chargers – check first.)

Obviously you will occasionally check the shores and the condition of the tarpaulin over the winter. The former need to be checked for even distribution of the load, the wedges being driven in further/pad spindles screwed up if necessary; the latter needs checking for damage and for places where it might be chafing the hull.

If the boat is otherwise in good condition on the technical front (ie no major overhaul or repair is outstanding), then the periodic checks described are all that is needed. But however long the winter may seem in one way, spring still comes too soon for some owners. When the March sunshine reactivates the 'sailing-bug' and boaters realize that in a mere four weeks (mid-April) the vessel should be hanging from the crane with all the spring tasks completed, then scenes of feverish activity follow at the laying-up sites. But that is precisely the time when ambient conditions are at their most unfavourable. Night frosts and warm days often prevent any painting because boat hulls – particularly those inside sheds – respond to major temperature variations by the formation of condensation that doesn't dry off for days or even weeks. If only a start had been made with the important overhauls in the mild autumn . . .

Don't wait till next spring

Painting, varnishing, GRP-work, underwater hull

Somehow it's a vicious circle. Nothing fits together. First it's too early, then it's too late. Season and weather, inclination and inability, laziness and necessity seem to be mutually exclusive, designed not to match.

If truth be told, most boatowners are quite pleased when the sailing season is over and the craft is safely ashore. Many things have been neglected over the summer. House and garden need attention, domestic events want attending to, friends need visiting, Christmas and New Year need celebrating. And then suddenly it's winter. Once autumn is over and the cold weather arrives, the boat has to wait until it's nearly too late. The time of going into winter quarters (ie mid-October to Christmas) would have been the best for doing all the maintenance work that now has to be done quickly, the success of which is now threatened by the dubious climatic conditions.

The pattern of the seasons in northern Europe seems indeed to be changing: analysed over a lengthy period, winter seems to start later and later. There is often mild autumn weather until at least the middle of November, which is followed by a short wintery spell; after this, there is another mild period until the end of the year. Typical winter weather with ice and snow often doesn't start until January, but then sometimes stays until well into March. Boaters who have properly recognized this pattern, and who start their overhaul of the vessel as soon as it is in its winter quarters, don't have the spring 'deadline' problem.

Any work requiring dry ground underfoot and mild temperatures should therefore be dealt with in the autumn. The owners of wooden-hulled boats should at least finish any sanding; some owners also do the varnishing, thus giving it plenty of time to harden. If you don't varnish until the spring, shortly before putting the boat back into the water, and if the vessel is then transported and re-launched in slings, there is a risk (at least with 'soft' single-pack varnish) of the slings leaving ugly marks. This of course also applies to wooden- or steel-hulled boats with coloured varnish/enamel, but the danger in their case is less because they are mostly painted with turps-based paint that has had a hardener added. However, it is even more important for these varnishes than for normal ones that they are applied at the highest possible air and hull temperatures, because the temperature has to be above a certain minimum for the chemical reaction between paint and hardener to produce a satisfactory result with the paint spread evenly and the surface shiny.

If synthetic-hulled boats need work done on the gel coat or the GRP, low humidity and high ambient temperature are particularly important, because deciding on the proportion of hardener to be added to the gel coat (or rather, the polyester resin) is an art in itself. Since almost every manufacturer of gel coats, resins and fillers expresses the amount of hardener as a percentage of the total mass of the mixture and, furthermore, this relates to a specific temperature, any deviation from the instructions carries the risk of the mixture hardening either much too quickly or not at all. If the boat is not found to be at the ideal application temperature at any time during wintering, recourse to external heat sources such as radiant heaters or high-wattage lamps is most strongly recommended to warm through the hull; then the material should be applied thoroughly.

That this is also easier in the autumn than in frosty winter weather is obvious.

Since most boatowners nowadays use nothing but modern underwater paints in lieu of the old 'wet' antifouling paint, even the hull can be painted in advance. Depending on the manufacturer and the application instructions on the tin, 'hard' antifouling paint may be exposed to the air for months, or indeed an unlimited length of time, without loss of effectiveness when the boat is re-launched. However, such paint still needs to be applied to a base that is dry. There are often dry periods in the autumn, but this job is therefore unsuitable in spring weather.

Major repairs, alterations and installations

The long months the boat is laid up is also the time for a lot of thinking and planning as to how your craft could be improved in appearance, comfort and safety. The boat-building and accessory industries are well aware of that: cunningly, they lure us to the major boat shows to show us what we could still bolt on, alter or convert. And then we have the water-pressurizing pump and the navigational computer, the auto-pilot and the solar-cell powered fan, the new loo, the halyard winch and the masthead light, all lying in the cellar at home because for the time being – February – it's much too uncomfortable on board to start fitting them. Then later, in March and April, there's pressure to get on with sanding and filling, painting and varnishing: there is no question now of undertaking complicated alterations and additions. And so the new equipment probably isn't commissioned until about May, when the family is already on board and everyone wants to get going, but the owner is head down in the bilge trying to get the new bilge pump to work. If you then discover that a particular bit of pipe is needed here, an extra teak console needs to be made for somewhere else, and you also badly need a special seal, you will find that neither the boat-engine fitter nor the carpenter nor the yard have any time for you because everyone else is there too.

It's much the same with the sailmaker. In the spring, even if he is in a position to let you have a new genoa, a roller-reefing outfit or a spray hood at short notice, he will certainly charge high-season prices. Whereas in the autumn – from October to Christmas – everyone is offering winter discounts.

So there is scarcely anything against starting early – in fact, everything to be said for it. There is really no place for panic, haste or stress when it comes to maintenance work. These feelings make you jittery, cause mistakes and harm the boat – which, anyway, will be a long way off being ready.

Recommissioning from winter quarters

At last we're there: the covering tarpaulin, neatly folded, is lying alongside the boat; the roof-structure timbers and rafters, marked and numbered for next time, are being stacked in the shed. Hull and deck gleam in the sun, cleaned once more to remove the last of the winter's dust and freshly polished, and the underwater hull glows with its coat of fresh paint. The proud vessel is ready to take to the water again. But let's play safe and check once more that it will float with the same assurance as it did last year, that the engine will start to take the boat from under the crane to its berth, and check whether any last preparations are needed before the crane takes over.

Our first concern must be for all the openings through the hull; these always represent a potential hazard with regard to the entry of sea water. Are all the hoses – sea-water cooling, cockpit drainage, deck drainage, galley sink, galley sea water pump, toilet flushing water, washbasin, toilet outflow, bilge pump, etc – connected to their sea cocks? Has any hose become porous or torn; are all the hose clips tight? After this, check that all sea cocks are closed, to be opened later in the water one at a time to check that all connections are tight. Now turn your attention to the prop shaft stern tube: can the shaft be turned in the bearing by hand in both directions, with no more than reasonable resistance? Is there play between shaft and bearing (shake at right angles to the shaft line)? Does this mean that – depending on the design – the stern gland has got to be renewed by inserting new O-rings or fresh tallow packing, or will tightening the large nut that applies pressure to the packing be enough? In the case of grease-lubricated stern tube bearings, has the grease gun been filled with the proper stiff stern tube grease and has the grease been fed into the bearing by turning the gun handle a few times? It's too late to do anything when the boat is in the water; if the stern gland leaks badly, the vessel has got to go back under the crane. The same check is applied to the rudder bearing, whose Teflon- or Tufnol-lining must be renewed if there is excessive play.

The following precautions should ensure that the auxiliary starts immediately, once the boat is in the water. Since the preparations for wintering included work on the cooling circuit and the fuel system, the impeller of the coolant pump should now be put back and the pump cover replaced, a new gasket being fitted. The diesel-engine fuel system must be vented. If done in accordance with the maker's instructions, using the hand pump and slacking back the various venting screws on filters and injection pump, this is usually a laborious chore. There is, on the other hand, no objection to turning the engine with the electric starter until it starts – operating the decompression lever if applicable. In conjunction with that, only one venting screw, and this the highest, the one on the fine filter, needs to be opened one turn. Even ashore in the cradle and without any cooling water, the engine can happily be run for a few seconds before being stopped again. But be careful – once the boat is back in the water, don't forget to open the engine-cooling sea cock before you start the engine again!

Before connecting the batteries to the on-board circuit, the switches to all electric equipment – made in the autumn to protect them against corrosion – should be broken again, or at least the battery master switch; otherwise, when the terminals are clipped on there will be an enormous spark.

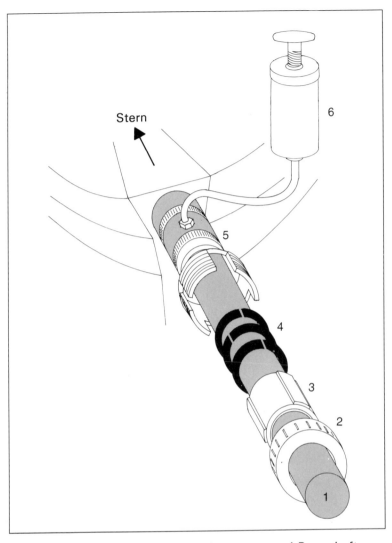

Stern tube with tallow packing and grease gun. 1 Prop shaft.
2 Packing-compressing nut. 3 Compressing ring. 4 Tallow
packing. 5 Rubber sleeve. 6 Grease gun.

The tallow packing has to be renewed as soon as an
excessive amount of sea water leaks in (normal amount about 1
drop/10secs). You do that by removing the old packing rings
after undoing the nut (2) and withdrawing the compressing ring
(3). The new rings of packing have to be cut to match the shaft
circumference. The butts should not be in line.

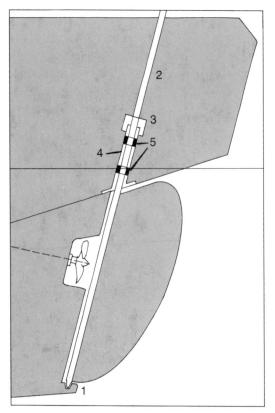

Rudder blade mounting of a long-keel yacht. 1 Skeg-iron or heel bearing. 2 Rudder stock. 3 Union-type nut. 4 Rudder tube. 5 Upper rudder bearing (bushes, Teflon or other synthetic material).

All bearings should be checked for excessive play, the bushes being renewed if necessary. There is usually a seal inside the union-type nut to stop water getting in.

The final checks before craning in are those on the underwater hull, and again the technical checks should be done first. Should your boat have an extra prop shaft bearing in the form of a shaft bracket, then that also has to have its – usually sea-water lubricated – synthetic-material bearing checked for

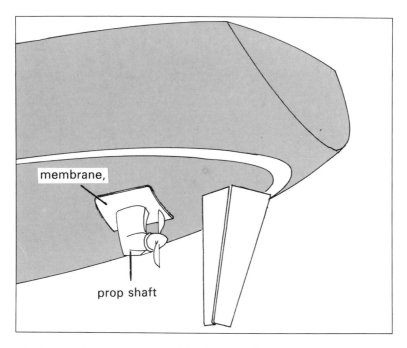

membrane,

prop shaft

The increasing popular 'saildrive' propulsion systems have many advantages. However, one component part requiring special attention is the large rubber membrane which acts as seal between prop shaft and underwater hull. This must be checked during laying up and' replaced if it looks porous or brittle.

play. In the case of the more and more frequently encountered 'saildrive' propulsion systems, the external rubber membrane acting as seal between prop shaft and hull must be checked most carefully for even the tiniest of cracks and any porous places and, if necessary, changed before the re-launch. Lastly, check the prop itself: if the blades are fixed, are they undamaged? If they're folding, do they fold and unfold freely? If it's an automatic CP-prop, does it get to its two end positions? If sacrificial anodes are fixed to the underwater hull, what is their condition? In particular, look at the one on the prop shaft: is there enough of it left to last another season?

There, that's the lot, I think. Your boat is safe to go in the water, ready for a new – and hopefully fine, refreshing, warm and harmonious – summer season. But wait – I nearly forgot! Take a little underwater paint along to the crane, and a brush. This is for those places on the hull and on the underside of the keel that you couldn't paint in winter quarters because of the cradle. Those five or so patches of paint that you are about to apply affectionately to your vessel hanging from the crane identify the true boat lover. That's *you*!

Index